Creative Plans For

YARD & GARDEN
STRUCTURES

Design HPT160004

74 Easy-To-Build Designs For Gazebos,
Sheds, Pool Houses, Playsets, Bridges and More!

HOME PLANNERS, LLC
Wholly owned by Hanley-Wood, LLC

TUCSON, ARIZONA

Contents

Designs by:
Matt DeBacker, Designer
Select Home Designs

Written by:
Connie Brown

Book Design by:
Jay C. Walsh, Graphic Designer

Photographs:
Front Cover:
©Werner G. Bertsch/Fotoconcept, Inc.
Back Cover:
©Frank Oberle/Photographic
Resources, Inc.
Antrim County Habitat for Humanity
Raef Grohne Photographer

Published by Home Planners, LLC
Wholly owned by Hanley-Wood, LLC

Editorial and Corporate Offices:
3275 West Ina Road, Suite 110
Tucson, Arizona 85741

Distribution Center:
29333 Lorie Lane
Wixom, Michigan 48393

President: Patricia Joseph
Editor in Chief: Jan Prideaux
Editor: Marian E. Haggard
Plans Editor: Ashleigh E. Muth
Production Artist: Tera Morriss

Library of Congress
Catalog Card Number: 00-108973

ISBN: 1-881995-82-6

10 9 8 7 6 5 4 3 2 1

On The Cover: This romantic gazebo will be the delight of your backyard parties. Finish as shown for a delicate Victorian look or use more rustic materials for an entirely different effect. For more information, see page 24.

Building Basics
For Yard & Garden Structures

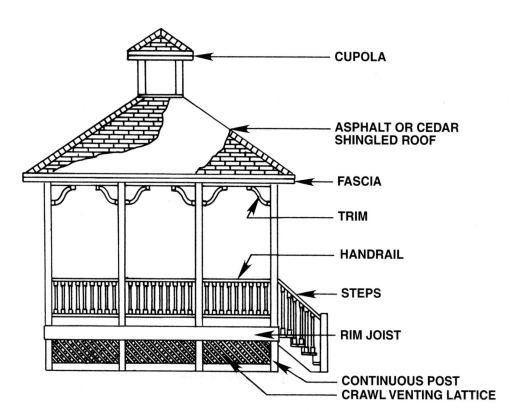

- CUPOLA
- ASPHALT OR CEDAR SHINGLED ROOF
- FASCIA
- TRIM
- HANDRAIL
- STEPS
- RIM JOIST
- CONTINUOUS POST
- CRAWL VENTING LATTICE

I magine . . . a playhouse for your children just outside your kitchen window; or your very own, free-standing shed for gardening or craft tools and supplies; or, a lovely garden swing nestled in a secluded, shady area by the side of your house. Or, on a more practical note, would your yard benefit from a compost bin, a pool cabana, or a bridge over a rocky or marshy area that is always such a problem?

Decorative, functional or just for fun, amenities and refinements *outside* your home can increase its living area and value—and provide hours of safe, relaxing outdoor living for every member of your family.

Projects such as those in this book are very doable! With an understanding of the basics, the right tools for the job, a set of our plans—plus an adequate supply of time and patience—you can turn a corner of your yard or garden into a useful and practical work area, or a charming and restful hideaway.

ADVANCE PLANNING
Project Selection

The first step, of course, is to decide on the project. Of all the possibilities, what does your home, your property, your family need the most: a garden swing,

a children's playset, a whimsical gazebo, or a practical tool shed?

If you already know what outdoor structure you want to add to your property (a lawn shed for garden supplies and equipment, perhaps) then move right along to the next easy step. Simply select the size and layout you prefer from the 19 plans for lawn sheds shown in this book. Then turn to page 124 for order information, and you're on your way.

> Remember, well-thought-out advance planning is crucial to a successful project.

Sometimes deciding what to build is not so easy. Keeping in mind the available space on your property and your budget, look through this book for ideas. The detailed descriptions of a wide variety of outdoor structures on pages 12–123 are sure to spark your imagination. Many designs have a variety of options, some just tailor-made for your family.

With all the possibilities fresh in your mind, take a slow walk around your property and decide which of

the outdoor structures is the best match in form and function to your family's needs and the space and budget you have available.

You'll need to consider if you have the time and expertise to build the project you've selected, or if you will need to involve a licensed contractor for all or part of the work.

Once all that's decided, refer to page 124 to order the plans you need and turn your thoughts to site selection.

Site Selection

Site selection depends on a number of things: what you are building, its purpose, who is going to use it, its accessibility and its appeal.

Location: If you decide to build a gazebo, it will likely become the focal point of your property. If you are constructing a playset, select an area that is visible from the house so you can watch the children. And, if your project is a compost bin, you probably want it located to the rear or side of your property, out of sight.

Drainage: If your property has moist areas, avoid them if you can. Don't place a playset or a garden swing in an area that remains damp for two or three days after a rain. The alternative is to provide a dry, firm base by adding sand and gravel fill under the project to aid the drainage of the site.

Utilities: Plan ahead for any utilities your project may require: electricity or water for sheds, gazebos and playhouses, or gas for heat or a grill. **Always call your local utilities providers for locations of underground cable and water lines, even if your project does not require utility connections.**

BUILDING BASICS

Building Permits

When your advance planning and site selection are complete, it's time to obtain the required building permits. Separate building permits are usually needed for each construction discipline: one for the structure, one for the electrical work, one for the plumbing, one for the heating and so on. Specific requirements for each vary from region to region across the country. Check with your local building officials *before you begin your project* to determine which permits you need. If your project is small, permits may not be required.

> Check with your local building officials
> *before you begin your project*
> to determine which permits you need.

Building Codes

Along with building permits come the codes which must be met. These codes are usually imposed by county or city governments. Codes are required to ensure that your project meets all standards for safety and construction methods. A local inspector will usually check the progress of your project at various stages, and there could be more than one inspector, depending on the utilities you incorporate.

Some of the regulated items the inspectors will check include: distance of project from property lines, handrail heights, stair construction, connection methods, footing sizes and depths, material being used, plumbing, electrical and mechanical requirements and neighborhood zoning regulations.

Site Plan

Creating a site plan, or detailed layout of the project on the property, is important when incorporating a new addition to an existing landscape. A site plan allows you to view in advance the effect a new structure will have when finished. It is important to conceptualize how the new addition blends in with property lines, utilities, other structures, permanent mature plants, land contours and roads. You also need to be certain of the visibility of the new structure from vantage points both outside and within your property lines. In addition, a site plan may be required by local building officials.

Tools Checklist

If you are an experienced do-it-yourselfer, you probably have most of the tools needed for any of the projects in this book. If this is your first project, compare the tools you have on hand to the list below. Most are available at rental shops, so you can have "the right tool for the job" without spending a lot of extra money right at first.

Gather together the tools you will need for your project *before you begin construction.* This simple rule is as important as having your building materials and lumber on site in the needed sizes and quantity before you start. The frustration and aggravation you eliminate will be well worth the time it takes to get organized before you begin.

Your basic tool list should include:

Brushes and rollers to apply finishes	Plumb bob
Carpenter's level	Power drill and screwdriver
Carpenter's square	Power jigsaw
Chalk line	Shovel
Chisel	Socket set
Circular saw	Tape measure
Framing angle	Tool belt
Hammer	Line level
Handsaw	Nail set
	Wheelbarrow (to move materials and to mix concrete)

Selecting Lumber

Each project in this book has a list of lumber and other building materials required. You will need to determine and select the type of wood you want to use. Many wood species are used for outdoor structures. Among the most common are: Redwood, Western Red Cedar, Douglas Fir, Spruce, Southern Yellow Pine, Northern Pine and Ponderosa Pine.

Lumber is available in a variety of grades depending on quality, strength and resistance to decay. For example, Redwood is graded as follows (listed from highest to lowest quality): Clear All Heart, Select Heart, Construction Heart and Merchantable Heart. Any of the last three grades are commonly used in outdoor construction projects.

One of the primary considerations in selecting the correct lumber for your project is to prevent the base structure from decaying. For this reason, lumber that is in contact with, or even in close proximity to, the ground must be decay-resistant. Select a resistant species and treat your lumber with a preservative before using it in your building or project.

> *Because of the chemicals used in its treatment, pressure-treated wood should not be used if it will come into direct contact with drinking water or food for humans or animals. Do not use pressure-treated wood for playsets.*

You might want to select pressure-treated wood, which is available from most lumber dealers and home centers. In pressure-treated wood, preservatives or fire-retardant chemicals are forced into the fibers of the lumber to protect and prolong its durability. Although pressure-treated wood seems an obvious choice, some precautions and decisions about its use are warranted. *Because of the chemicals used in its treatment, pressure-treated wood should not be used if it will come into direct contact with drinking water or food for humans or animals. Do not use pressure-treated wood for playsets.* Further precautions include: do not use boards with a visible chemical residue; wear a mask and goggles when sawing treated wood; do not burn treated wood; and sweep up and safely dispose of all sawdust and wood scraps. Check with your lumber supplier for additional restrictions and precautions.

Choose a lumber dealer you can rely on to assist you with wood selection—one who will be familiar with the lumber commonly used in your area for outdoor projects. Be sure what you want is available locally. If you desire a wood type that is not normally in stock in your part of the country, you'll pay much more to acquire it.

SITE PREPARATION

At last, it's time to begin! You've selected the site according to your observations and site plan; you've obtained complete project plans; you've secured all permits; and you've gathered together all code-approved materials and required tools. Now, to help assure success, follow these important steps so construction will proceed quickly and without too many hitches.

Drainage: This is an important word to remember when you begin construction. Water must drain away from the foundation or it will pool on structural supports, eventually rotting and weakening them. And, water-saturated soil beneath footings may not remain firm enough to support the structure.

The easiest way to supply drainage is to slope the

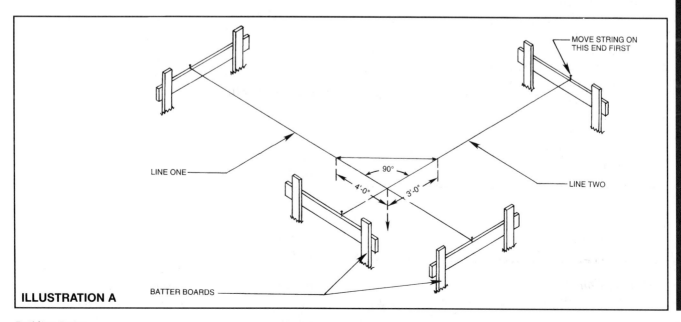

ILLUSTRATION A

MOVE STRING ON THIS END FIRST

LINE ONE

LINE TWO

90°

4'-0" 3'-0"

BATTER BOARDS

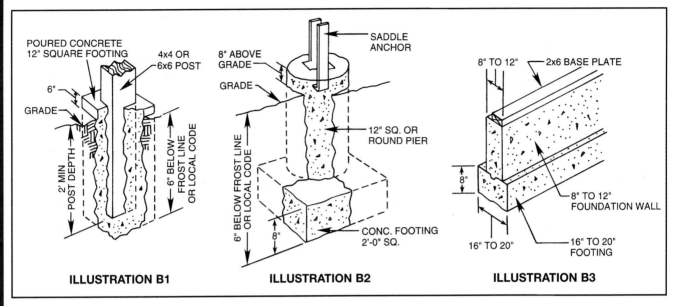

ILLUSTRATION B1   **ILLUSTRATION B2**   **ILLUSTRATION B3**

ground away from your structure so water will run off naturally. If the ground does not slope naturally, dig a drainage channel or channels to carry water away. Notice where water runoff flows naturally and install trenches there.

If runoff is light, dig trenches about 1 foot deep and line with 1 to 2 inches of gravel. If possible, direct the runoff downhill into irrigation wells for trees and shrubs. This form of water harvesting has dual benefits: it takes care of excess water and it supplies plants with needed moisture.

If runoff is heavy, further engineering will be required, such as laying perforated pipe, or lining the trenches with concrete. Consult with an architect or engineer to see if these or additional methods are required to handle heavy runoff.

Remove weeds and turf: Getting weeds out of the way before you begin to build makes construction easier. Hoe or pull out weeds in small areas. In larger areas, a small cultivator can be used to turn over the soil. Keep cultivation shallow or weed seeds will be brought up to the soil surface to germinate.

To prevent future weed growth, lay down heavy black plastic sheeting (at least 6 mils thick). Newly available "fabric mulch" is also good for this purpose. It prevents weed growth, yet allows water to pass through and soak into the soil, which results in less runoff downgrade. Cover the sheeting or mulch with about 2 inches of pea gravel to hold it in place.

PROJECT LAYOUT

A simple surveying procedure allows you to be sure your project will be built square, with true 90-degree angles. Batter boards are used to square the starting corner of your project. This corner could be the outside wall of the foundation or the center point of your first post. The first step is to construct a right triangle using the "3-4-5 Method" described below. (Actually, any multiple of 3-4-5, such as 6-8-10, or 12-16-20 will work—the larger the better.)

The 3-4-5 Method

Using stakes and string, run a line (Line One) parallel to what you have determined will be the front of your project. Install batter boards as shown in *Illustration A* (see page 5) and attach string. Be sure the batter boards are far enough apart to build your project between. Install a second set of batter boards perpendicular to Line One and attach Line Two. Using a length of string or a measuring tape, measure 4 feet along Line One from the point where it intersects Line Two. Mark that point with a piece of string that will slide. Measure 3 feet along Line Two from the Line One/Line Two intersection point and mark it with a piece of string that will slide. Next, measure 3 feet along Line Two from the Line One/Line Two intersection and mark it in the same manner. Now, measure the distance across from the string you tied to Line One to the string on Line Two. The corner is exactly square when this distance is five feet.

Adjust the string on the far end of Line Two and slide the string on Line One until the measurements equal the correct ratio. Double-check the accuracy by placing a carpenter's square in the corner. This process will establish a point with a perfect 90-degree angle from which to begin building your project. Regardless of where the point is it will become the main reference point for the entire project.

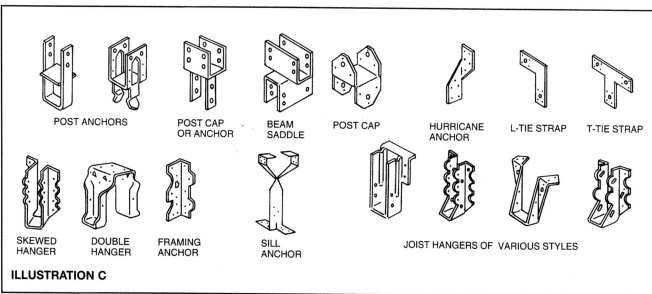

POST ANCHORS   POST CAP OR ANCHOR   BEAM SADDLE   POST CAP   HURRICANE ANCHOR   L-TIE STRAP   T-TIE STRAP

SKEWED HANGER   DOUBLE HANGER   FRAMING ANCHOR   SILL ANCHOR   JOIST HANGERS OF VARIOUS STYLES

ILLUSTRATION C

FOUNDATIONS, FOOTINGS AND PIERS

A poor foundation can ruin even the best project. *Illustration B* presents three options for a foundation, using piers and a poured concrete wall on a footer. Other methods include a concrete block foundation wall, or even placing your structure directly on pre-cast concrete piers.

Local codes vary in requirements for footing sizes and depths. If you are in an area where the ground freezes, footings must be placed at the code-recommended depth below natural level. *Be sure to check the codes in your area before installing the footings for your project.*

> *Be sure to check the codes in your area before installing the footings for your project.*

Piers, footings and foundations are the base of any project. Piers are formed from concrete, either pre-cast or "pour-your-own." To pour your own, either build your own forms from lumber, or use the ready-made forms of wax-impregnated cardboard, available in cylinder or block shapes at local home-improvement or lumber supply stores.

Foundation walls are commonly made by pouring the footer in a ditch to the required depth (8 to 12 inches), and then building forms. The foundation wall is poured on top of the footing. An optional method is to set a block foundation wall on top of the footing. Pre-cast piers are available in various sizes and with drift-pin connections. These can be set on grade or sunken into the ground, depending on the type you select.

ATTACH PROJECT TO FOUNDATION

Whether your project is sitting on posts or a foundation wall, all wood within 12 inches of the soil should be treated as required by most codes. *Illustrations B1 and B2* show the two most common ways to attach a post to a footing or pier. By setting metal connectors in poured concrete you will create a strong connection less susceptible to wood rot than simply sinking a post in concrete. All connectors should be of the highest quality 16- to 18-gauge hot-dipped galvanized steel. Ensure that all nails, bolts, nuts and other fittings exposed to the elements are also of galvanized steel.

Illustration B3 shows the base plate on the top of the foundation wall secured with anchor bolts. This plate will support the floor joist.

Many additional foundation options are available, such as slab flooring with anchor ties, block walls and others. The one you need will be indicated in the detailed set of plans for each project.

Leveling Post Height

If you are pouring a foundation wall or laying block, the top should be perfectly level for placing the sill plate. Since posts set in or on top of a footing or pier may vary in height, follow these guidelines. Use a post 6 inches longer than needed to allow for variations. After the concrete has set, string a level line to find the top of the post height needed for your project. Level the posts and cut to the same height prior to attaching floor joists or beams.

Making Framing Connections

Joists, rafters and even sill plate connections can be made stronger by using manufactured metal framing devices. *Illustration C* shows a variety of connectors and their applications. Other connectors are available which are easy to install and provide a strong connection.

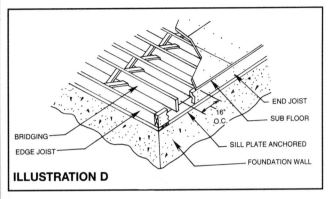

BRIDGING · EDGE JOIST · END JOIST · SUB FLOOR · SILL PLATE ANCHORED · FOUNDATION WALL · 16" O.C.

ILLUSTRATION D

STANDARD FLOOR CONSTRUCTION

Of all possible structural systems, platform framing is the easiest and most common method used. The entire floor frame is constructed first, including the subflooring, as in *Illustration D*. In this way, the floor surface serves as a platform for the structure's walls. If a slab is poured, it then acts as the platform.

To construct a floor frame, a sill plate is attached to the foundation wall with anchor bolts. Then the header joists and edge joists are set upright and nailed to the sill plate. Header, edge and regular joists are all constructed using the same size lumber. The sill plate will usually be a 2x6. Floor joists are normally placed 16 inches on center with splices only occurring above a beam. The subflooring extends to the edges of the floor framing structure.

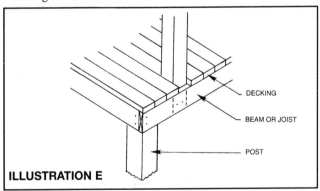

DECKING · BEAM OR JOIST · POST

ILLUSTRATION E

If you are building a gazebo or other structure using 5x4 or 5x2 decking, the joists may attach to the posts or beams with the decking extended to the edge. It may also be modified for railings or columns, as shown in *Illustration E*.

Structural Bracing

Additional bracing can be provided with blocking or cross-bridging. "Blocking" uses boards the same dimension as the joists, placed between the joists for added support. "Cross-bridging" uses 2x3s or 2x4s placed in an X pattern between joists for added support. If blocking boards are cut precisely to size before joists

are installed, they can serve as a measure to ensure correct spacing between joists. Stagger the blocking pattern to make it easier to install.

Be sure all joists are installed at the same level. Because the actual project flooring goes on top of the joists, they must be the same height or the surface of the floor will be uneven. To check, place a line over the joists and pull it tight. It will be easy to tell which joists are too high or too low and need to be adjusted.

Splicing Joists

Joists, like beams, must be spliced when they do not span the entire distance between beams. Splice only above a beam to ensure needed support. Use a wood or metal cleat, or overlap the joist at the beam. Extend the joint 8 inches or more beyond the sides of each beam to increase the strength of the junction and to allow room for the splice.

If the joist spans over 8 feet, apply a cross-brace or blocking to prevent twisting. The longer the distance, the more likely the joist is to twist. If the floor span of your project is 8 feet or less, the end headers normally provide enough support so that cross-bracing is not required. Use blocking for added support for joists that are 2x4, 2x6 or 2x8, but for joists that are 2x10 or larger, install wood or metal cross bracing.

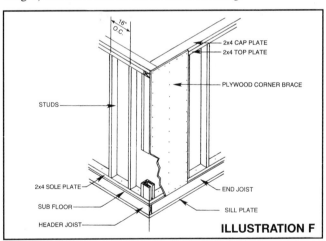

16" O.C. · 2x4 CAP PLATE · 2x4 TOP PLATE · PLYWOOD CORNER BRACE · STUDS · 2x4 SOLE PLATE · SUB FLOOR · HEADER JOIST · END JOIST · SILL PLATE

ILLUSTRATION F

STANDARD WALL CONSTRUCTION

In platform framing, exterior walls and interior partitions have a single 2x4-plate (2x6 when studs are 2x6s) that rests on the subfloor. This is called the bottom or sole plate. The top of the walls have a doubled plate called the top plate, or cap plate, that supports ceiling joists, and, in most cases, roof rafters. The walls of a structure usually are built lying flat on the subfloor, then raised into position in one section. Wall studs are also normally placed 16 inches on center, but if 2x6 studs are used, then 24 inches on center may be acceptable.

There are a number of ways to construct the corner post. The method shown in *Illustration F* is one of the most common. Also shown is a sheet of exterior plywood at the corner. This is used as corner bracing. There are other methods, such as a 2x4 notched at a 45-degree angle, or metal **X** bracing, but using plywood is the easiest and fastest method. For small structures with ⅝ inch T-111 siding, or equal, this could also serve as the needed corner bracing and is sufficient for most codes.

Prior to starting the wall construction, be sure to verify all rough opening sizes for doors, windows, etc. All headers above the doors and windows are constructed of 2x material, which is really 1½ inch thick. With two 2x6s or 2x8s with a ½ inch plywood spacer, you can build a header to support almost any window or door span for the projects in this book.

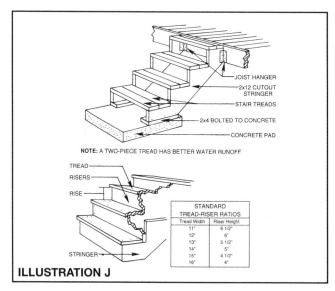

NOTE: A TWO-PIECE TREAD HAS BETTER WATER RUNOFF

STANDARD TREAD-RISER RATIOS	
Tread Width	Riser Height
11"	6 1/2"
12"	6"
13"	5 1/2"
14"	5"
15"	4 1/2"
16"	4"

ILLUSTRATION J

gable (*Illustration G*) and the hip (*Illustration H*). For garden-amenity structures, other styles are also used, such as a shed roof or gambrel roof, plus variations and combinations of each style.

There are five roof-framing terms you should know which are used in calculating rafter length: span, rise, run, pitch and pitch line, as shown in *Illustration I*. To construct a roof you will need to use a rafter square, available from local suppliers. Get either a metal angle or a triangular square. The least expensive model is a plastic triangular square. It comes with instructions on how to use it to measure rafters, cut angles and cut "the bird's mouth," which is the part that sits on the wall cap plate. Because cutting the roof rafters is probably the most difficult task involved in building a garden structure, the rafter square is the most useful tool you can have.

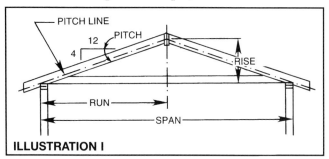

ILLUSTRATION I

ROOF FRAMING

Up to the cap plate or top plate, the method of construction depends on the type of framing system used. *Above* the cap plate, the method of construction depends mainly on the style of the roof indicated for the structure.

Two structures built from identical plans can look considerably different when only the style of the roof is changed. The two most common roof styles are the

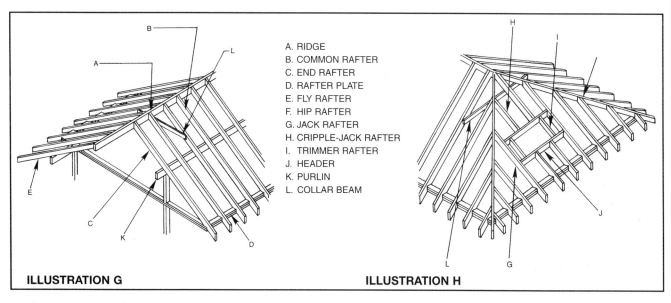

A. RIDGE
B. COMMON RAFTER
C. END RAFTER
D. RAFTER PLATE
E. FLY RAFTER
F. HIP RAFTER
G. JACK RAFTER
H. CRIPPLE-JACK RAFTER
I. TRIMMER RAFTER
J. HEADER
K. PURLIN
L. COLLAR BEAM

ILLUSTRATION G

ILLUSTRATION H

STAIRS AND STEPS

Most outdoor projects require stairs and steps to provide exits to ground level. Stairs are composed of the *tread,* the surface you walk on, and the *riser,* the vertical distance between steps. Stairs are usually 4-, 5- or 6-feet wide. It is important that you retain a constant *riser-to-tread* ratio. This ensures an equal distance between steps to avoid missteps and stumbles. A common riser-to-tread ratio is 6:12, which can be built by using two 2x6 treads and a 2x6 riser. For example, if the width of the tread is 12 inches, the next step should "rise" 6 inches.

The supports to which the steps are attached are called *stair stringers* or *carriage,* usually built from a 2x12. Steps can also be constructed as a single step from floor to ground, or from one floor level to another. Some steps are constructed as a separate level, a kind of continuous step, from one floor level to another. *Illustration J* shows the options for stringers and treads, plus a chart indicating standard tread-riser ratios.

INSULATION

If you are going to heat or cool your structure, you may want to insulate the walls and ceiling. If so, the normal wall insulation is R-19 in cold climates, with R-38 for the ceiling. R-values vary according to climate, so check with your local supplier for the requirements in your area.

GLOSSARY

Anchor bolt: A device for connecting wood members to concrete or masonry.

Blocking: Used for added support for floor joists and to prevent twisting.

Balustrade: A complete handrail assembly. Includes rails, balusters, subrails and fillets.

Batter board: Simple wooden forms used early in construction to mark the corners of the structure and the height of foundation walls.

Beam: A horizontal framing member of wood or steel, no less than 5 inches thick and at least 2 inches wider than it is thick.

Board: Any piece of lumber more than 1 inch wide, but less than 2 inches wide in thickness.

Common rafter: Any of several identical structural members of a roof that run at right angles to walls and end at right angles to main roof framing members.

Concrete: A mixture of cement, sand, gravel and water.

Cross-bridging: Diagonal wood braces that form an X between floor joists to prevent twisting.

Drip edge: A strip of metal used to protect the edges of a roof structure from water damage.

Drywall: A method of covering wall and ceiling surfaces with dry materials, rather than wet materials such as plaster. Refers primarily to the application of gypsum wallboard, also called drywall.

Edge joist: The outer joist of a floor or ceiling system that runs parallel to other joists. See *header joist.*

Foundation: The part of a building that rests on a footing and supports all of the structure above it.

Frame: The wood skeleton of a building. Also called framing.

Header: Any structural wood member used across the ends of an opening to support the cut ends of shortened framing members in a floor, wall or roof.

Header joist: The outer joist of a floor or ceiling system that runs across other joists. See *edge joist.*

Joist: A horizontal structural member that, together with other similar members, supports a floor or ceiling system.

O.C.: Abbreviation for "On Center," a measurement from one center line to the next, usually of structural members.

Ridgeboard: The horizontal board at the ridge to which the top ends of rafters are attached. Also called a "ridge beam" or "ridge pole."

Plans You Can Build
For Yard & Garden Structures

Building a beautiful or practical outdoor addition in your yard or garden should be like adding icing to a cake. A something-extra, value-added, just-for-fun project from concept through completion. Whether you built your home or had it built—just moved in or have been there for years—take a look around with a "wish list" in mind. Given your lifestyle, what would you and your family use most? A garden swing? A romantic gazebo? A potting shed? Or a just-what-you've-always-wanted shed for tools?

On the following pages are illustrations for 74 projects, some practical, some whimsical, but all designed to enhance your lifestyle and make creative use of your outdoor areas. Complete construction blueprints are available for you to order for each project. (The Compost Bin, on page 60, has complete instructions right in the book!) All are ready for you to build or have a professional contractor build for you. Each is easily adaptable to almost any style or type of home or outdoor area.

Blueprint packages include everything you or your contractor will need to complete these projects—frontal sheet, materials list, floor plan, framing plan, and where needed, elevations. In addition, Home Planners offers a Gazebo Construction Details package which provides additional information for building gazebos, as well as a Standard Construction Details package which gives advice on basic building techniques. (See page 124 for more information.)

Take your time as you look through the following pages. Imagine how each project shown would look in your yard or garden, and the enjoyment and convenience your family would receive. When you've decided on a project, simply turn to page 124 for order information. We'll rush the plans to you and answer any questions you may have.

Wedding Bells
Plan HPT160001

Width: 11'-6"
Depth: 12'-0"

FLOOR PLAN

Features At A Glance:

- *Unique Appearance*
- *Attractively Spacious*
- *Easy to Build*

See page 124 to order complete construction drawings for this plan.

Imagine the big day—a wedding set in the comfort and familiarity of your own backyard. Enchanting and unforgettably romantic, this memorable gazebo is a splendid addition to any garden scene. Family and friends will be dazzled by this 106-square-foot structure—large enough to accommodate a wedding party or a trio of musicians.

Build this fine design with unpainted, treated materials to give the feeling of being in a wooded glade, or paint it white for a storybook atmosphere. Simple yet elegant, this gazebo will enhance the scenery and add to the allure of any private garden. Benches may be added to offer outdoor covered seating on breezy summer nights.

Brisk Autumn Charmer
Plan HPT160002

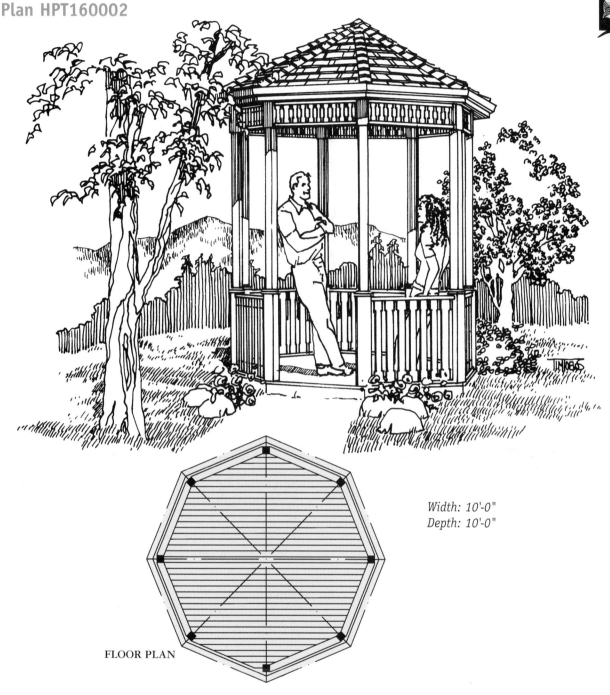

Width: 10'-0"
Depth: 10'-0"

FLOOR PLAN

Features At A Glance:

- *Simple Design*
- *Rustic Appearance*
- *Add Extras*

See page 124 to order complete construction drawings for this plan.

Simple, yet brisk—this charming gazebo offers a sheltered openness to any yard display. You can keep it simple and have it blend with any landscape, or add a bit of pre-cut scroll work and—presto! you have a fariytale in your own backyard. With 71 square feet, this gazebo is petite, yet elegantly rustic for the countryside setting. It provides a haven and decorative motif to any garden or outdoor arrangement.

Add a table and chairs and enjoy afternoon lemonade or tea over a game of cards. Or build in a wraparound bench and imitate the scene from *The Sound of Music*! Certainly, this structure will encourage outdoor leisure almost any time of the year.

Neo-Classic Gazebo
Plan HPT160003

Features At A Glance:

- *Classic Lines*
- *Spacious*
- *Complements Many Housing Styles*

See page 124 to order complete construction drawings for this plan.

Best suited for larger lots—at least a half acre—this gazebo provides a prime spot for entertaining. At 144-plus square feet of decking, it has as much surface space as the average family room. And, topping out at just under 17½ feet, it's as tall as a one-story house!

Boasting many neo-classic features—perfect proportions, columns and bases— it blends well with a variety of housing styles: Cape, Georgian, farmhouse and others. The cupola is an added touch that lets light flow to the decking below. Cedar or redwood would be a good choice for building materials.

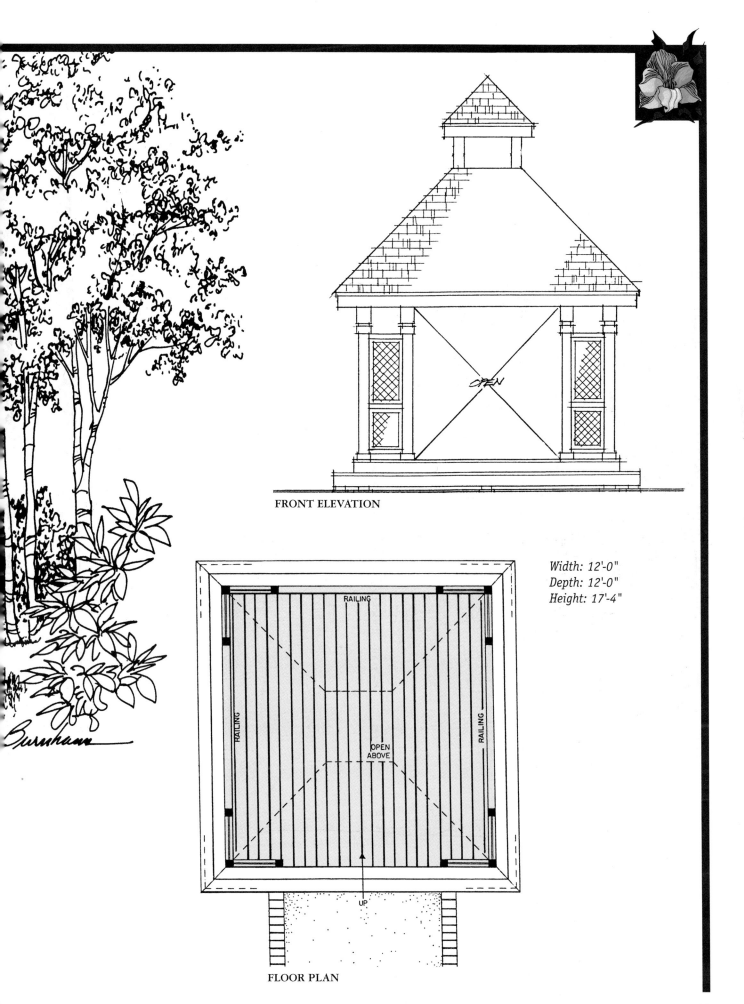

FRONT ELEVATION

OPEN

Width: 12'-0"
Depth: 12'-0"
Height: 17'-4"

RAILING

RAILING

RAILING

OPEN
ABOVE

UP

FLOOR PLAN

American Bandstand
Plan HPT160004

Features At A Glance:

- *Easy Square Shape*
- *Large Floor Area*
- *Accommodates Crawlspace*

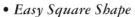

See page 124 to order complete construction drawings for this plan.

Dance the night away in this double-entrance, pass-through-style gazebo. By day, the open-air construction provides a clear view in all directions. The large floor area of 256 square feet seats 12 to 16 people comfortably or nicely accommodates musicians or entertainers for a lawn party. The decorative cupola can be lowered, louvered or removed to create just the appearance you want. Or, add an antique weathervane just for fun.

This gazebo has five steps up, which gives it a large crawlspace for access to any added utilities. Its square shape allows for simple cutting and floor framing, plus easy assembly of the roof frame. The trim and handrails are simple to construct or modify to achieve several different design effects.

The trim and handrails are simple to construct or modify to achieve several different design effects.

SIDE ELEVATION

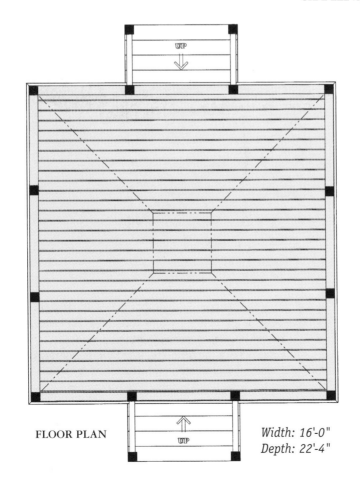

FLOOR PLAN

Width: 16'-0"
Depth: 22'-4"

American Classic
Plan HPT160005

Features At A Glance:

- *Adapts to a Variety of Styles*
- *Large Floor Area*
- *Basic Design*

See page 124 to order complete construction drawings for this plan.

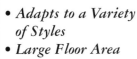

This all-American single-entrance gazebo is simple to construct and easy to adapt to a variety of styles. All materials are available in most areas with no special cutting for trim or rails. This gazebo is distinguished by its simple design and large floor area. The traditional eight-sided configuration and overall area of approximately 181 square feet allow for the placement of furniture with ample seating for 8 to 10 people.

Build as shown, or modify the trim and railings to give a totally different appearance. If multiple entrance/exit access is desired, simply eliminate the rails as needed. Access to the ground is a single step, which could be easily modified for a low ramp.

This gazebo is distinguished by its simple design and large floor area.

FRONT ELEVATION

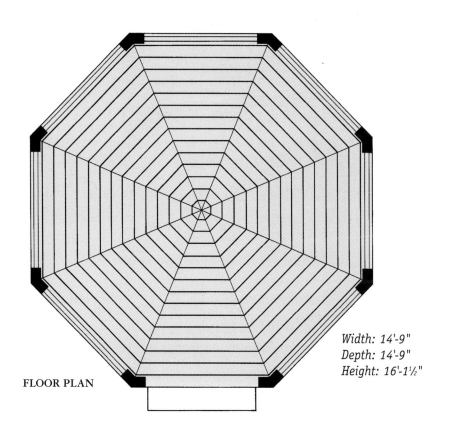

FLOOR PLAN

Width: 14'-9"
Depth: 14'-9"
Height: 16'-1½"

Once Upon A Time
Plan HPT160006

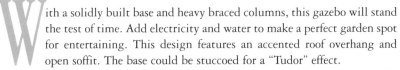

Features At A Glance:

- *Solid Base*
- *Vented Crawlspace*
- *Benches for Increased Seating*

See page 124 to order complete construction drawings for this plan.

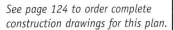

With a solidly built base and heavy braced columns, this gazebo will stand the test of time. Add electricity and water to make a perfect garden spot for entertaining. This design features an accented roof overhang and open soffit. The base could be stuccoed for a "Tudor" effect.

This two-step-up structure has a vented crawlspace in the base to give quick access to any added utilities. The floor area is approximately 181 square feet and will accommodate 8 to 10 people in standard chairs. The double entrance can be modified to a single entrance, with benches added to increase seating to twenty-one.

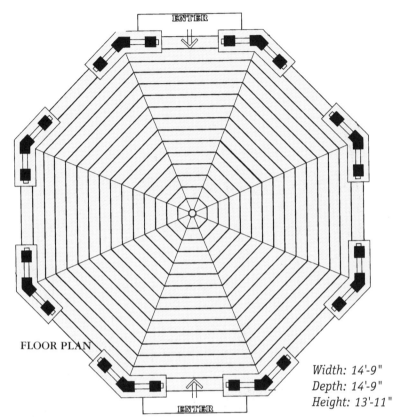

ENTER

FLOOR PLAN

Width: 14'-9"
Depth: 14'-9"
Height: 13'-11"

ENTER

The double
entrance can be
modified to a single
entrance, with
benches added to
increase seating to
twenty-one.

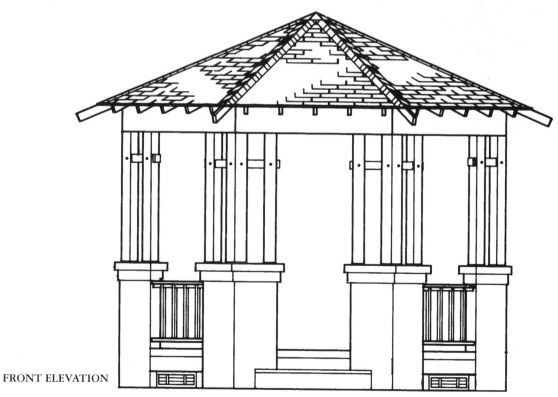

FRONT ELEVATION

Trellis-Go-Round
Plan HPT160007

Features At A Glance:

- *Trellis Roof*
- *Simple to Construct*
- *Garden Options*

See page 124 to order complete construction drawings for this plan.

Up, down and green all around! Light and airy, the unique trellis roof of this innovative single-entrance gazebo is just waiting for your favorite perennial vines. To extend the green-all-around look, modify the railings to a lattice pattern and train vines or grapes—or roses, for a splash of color—to experience nature all around you. The inset corners of the design provide plenty of space for planting. Simple lines make this delightful gazebo easy to construct, with no cumbersome cutting or gingerbread. The large area—128 square feet—provides built-in seating for 9 people. This flexible design could be modified to a closed roof with any standard roof sheathing and shingles, and the single entrance design can be altered to accommodate multiple entrances.

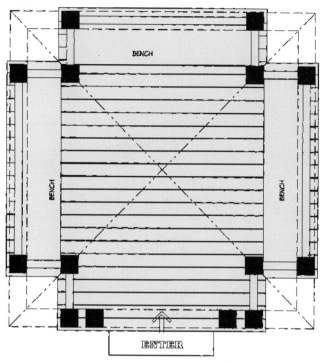

FLOOR PLAN

The inset corners of the design provide plenty of space for planting.

Width: 12'-0"
Depth: 12'-0"
Height: 13'-0"

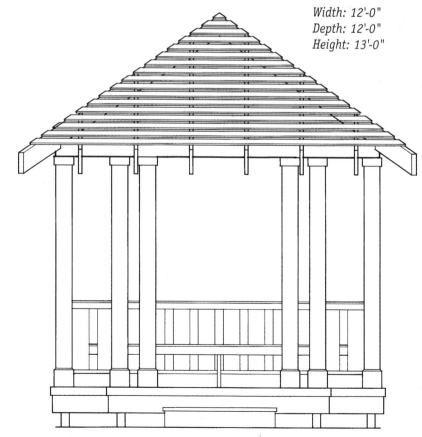

FRONT ELEVATION

The Ornament
Plan HPT160008

R. GERMANA

Features At A Glance:

- *Outstanding Focal Point*
- *Easy to Build*
- *Large Floor Area*

See page 124 to order complete construction drawings for this plan.

Reflecting the image "gingerbread" is intended to convey, the delightful gazebo shown will be the focal point of your landscape . . .the icing on the cake . . . the star atop the holiday tree! The floor area of nearly 120 square feet is large enough for a table and 4 to 6 chairs. Or, add built-in benches to increase the seating capacity to accommodate 16 people.

Painted white with pink asphalt roof shingles, this gazebo has a cool summery appearance. Or, you can build it with unpainted, treated materials and cedar shake shingles for an entirely different effect. Either exterior design will provide an outstanding setting for years of outdoor relaxation and entertainment. The jaunty cupola complete with spire adds a stately look to this single-entrance structure. The plans also include an optional arbor, which can be incorporated into the entrance of the gazebo.

Reflecting the image "gingerbread" is intended to convey, the delightful gazebo shown will be the focal point of your landscape.

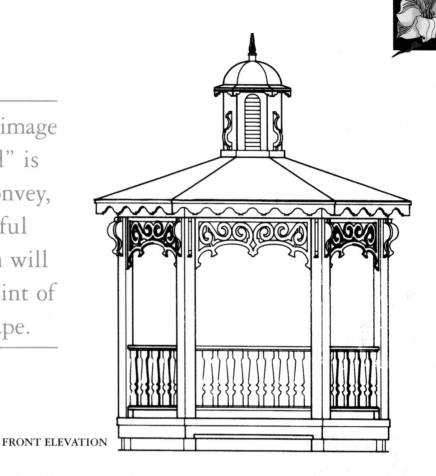

FRONT ELEVATION

Width: 11'-8"
Depth: 11'-8"
Height: 17'-5"

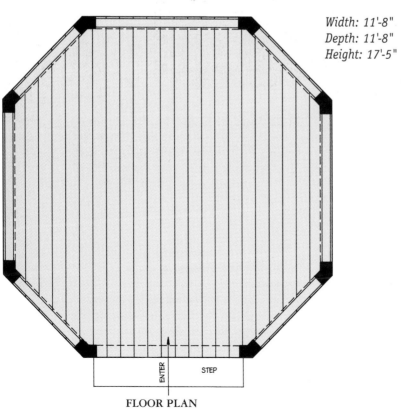

ENTER   STEP

FLOOR PLAN

Kaleidoscope
Plan HPT160009

Features At A Glance:

- *Operable Louvers*
- *Masonry Base*
- *Optional Copper Cover*

See page 124 to order complete construction drawings for this plan.

Shining copper on the cupola and shimmering glass windows all around enhance this double-entrance gazebo with dancing light and color. The many windows allow natural light to engulf the interior, making it a perfect studio. Easy to heat and cool, this gazebo contains operable louvers in the cupola to increase the flow of air. An exhaust fan could be added to the cupola to further maximize air flow.

The masonry base with brick steps gives the structure a definite feeling of both elegance and permanence. The roof structure is made from standard framing materials with the cupola adorned with a copper cover. If cost is a factor, the cupola roof could be made of asphalt shingles and the glass windows could be eliminated.

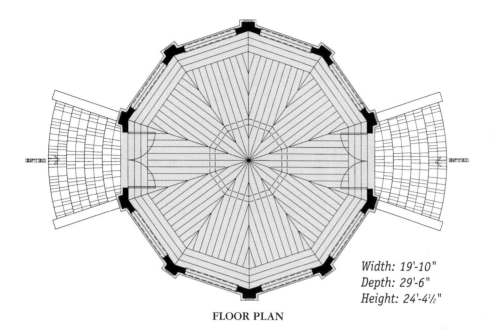

FLOOR PLAN

Width: 19'-10"
Depth: 29'-6"
Height: 24'-4½"

The masonry base with brick steps gives the structure a definite feeling of both elegance and permanence.

FRONT ELEVATION

Country Garden
Plan HPT160010

Features At A Glance:

- *Built-in Planters*
- *Large Area*
- *Open-Air Lattice Work*

See page 124 to order complete construction drawings for this plan.

The built-in planters and open roof areas of this multiple-entrance gazebo make this design a gardener's dream-come-true. The open roof allows sun and rain ample access to the planters and gives the structure a definite country-garden effect. Built with or without a cupola, the open latticework in the walls and roof complements a wide variety of landscapes and home designs. A creative gardener will soon enhance this charming gazebo with a wealth of plants and vines. Tuck a bird bath or bubbling fountain into a corner to further the garden setting. The large footprint—256 square feet—ensures that both you and nature have plenty of room to share all that this gazebo has to offer. It easily accommodates a table and chairs when you invite your guests to this outdoor hideaway.

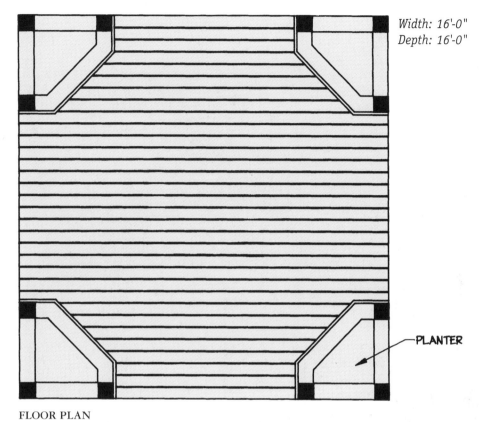

Width: 16'-0"
Depth: 16'-0"

PLANTER

FLOOR PLAN

A creative gardener will soon enhance this charming gazebo with a wealth of plants and vines.

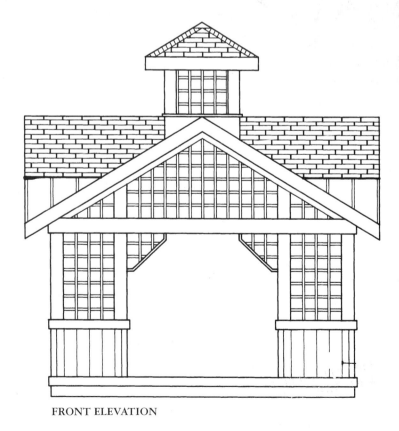

FRONT ELEVATION

Star Struck

Plan HPT160011

Features At A Glance:

- *Large Capacity*
- *Unique Appearance*
- *Easy to Modify*

See page 124 to order complete construction drawings for this plan.

Designed for serious entertaining, the size alone—162 square feet—lets you know this gazebo is unique. The star-lattice railing design, built-in benches and raised center roof with accent trim make this structure as practical as it is attractive. Large enough for small parties, there is built-in seating for about 12 people and enough floor area for another 5 to 10. Ideal for entertaining, the addition of lights and a wet bar make this design an important extension of any home.

The rooflines and overhang can be modified to give an Oriental effect, or removed completely to give a carousel-like appearance. Although this double-entrance, pass-through gazebo looks complicated, it is fairly simple to build with the right tools and materials.

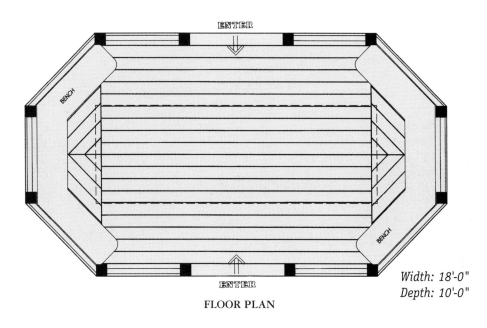

ENTER
↓

BENCH

BENCH

ENTER
↑

Width: 18'-0"
Depth: 10'-0"

FLOOR PLAN

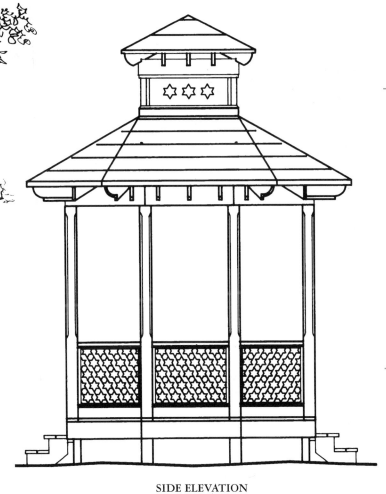

SIDE ELEVATION

The rooflines and overhang can be modified to give an Oriental effect, or removed completely to give a carousel-like appearance.

Graceful Garden
Plan HPT160012

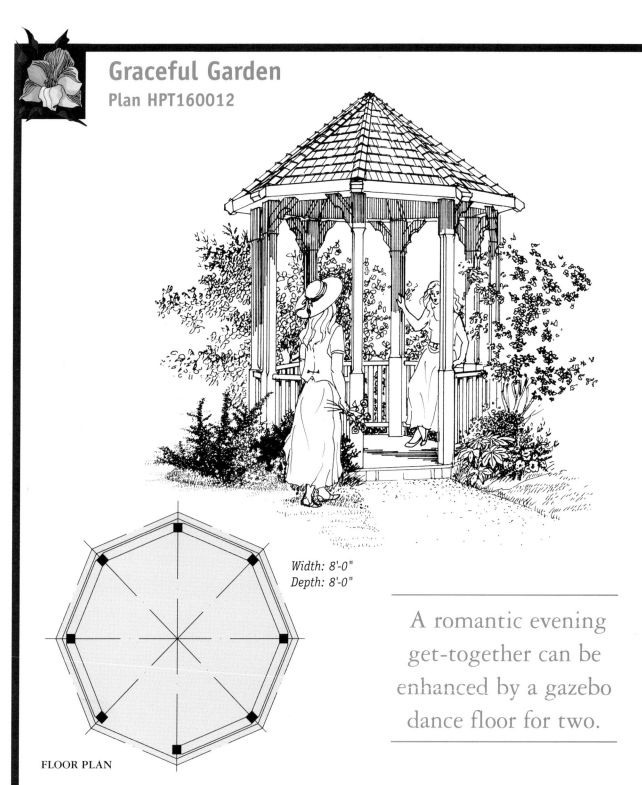

Width: 8'-0"
Depth: 8'-0"

FLOOR PLAN

A romantic evening
get-together can be
enhanced by a gazebo
dance floor for two.

Features At A Glance:

- *Graceful Accents*
- *Romantic Dance Floor*
- *Stylish Display*

*See page 124 to order complete
construction drawings for this plan.*

A graceful ambiance accents the inner and outer structure of this charming garden gazebo. Host a summertime picnic and enjoy the alluring shade provided, while you mingle with friends and family. A romantic evening get-together can be enhanced by a gazebo dance floor for two, decorated with hanging Chinese lanterns. Or you can set up a table and let the kids enjoy outdoor arts and crafts, safe from the threat of blistering summertime sunburns. With an endless number of possibilities, this outdoor display is both a useful and stylish addition to any home landscape.

Make It Your Own
Plan HPT160013

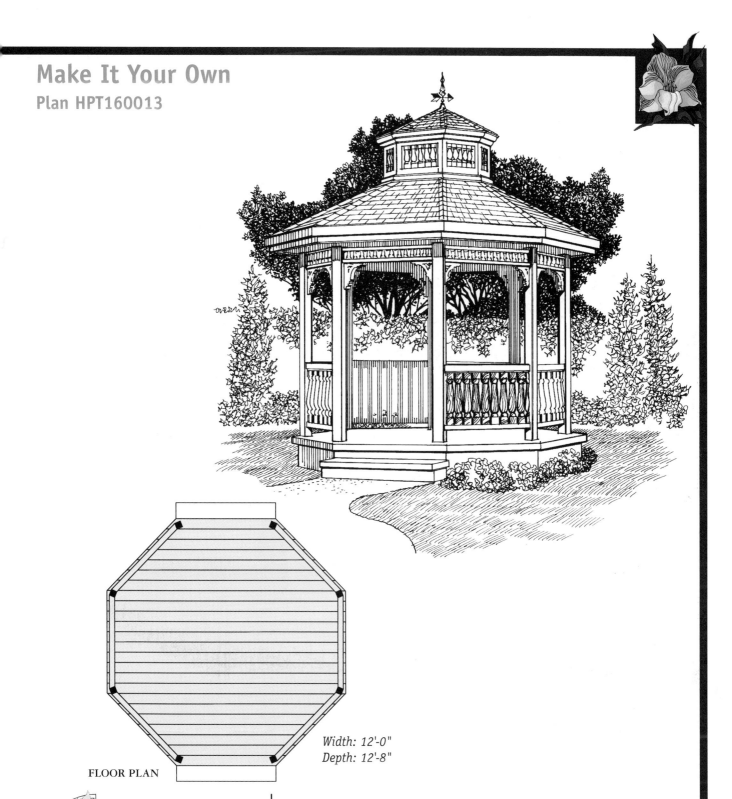

FLOOR PLAN

Width: 12'-0"
Depth: 12'-8"

Features At A Glance:

- *Victorian Accents*
- *Elegant Weathervane*
- *Outdoor Entertainment*

See page 124 to order complete construction drawings for this plan.

Victorian on a small scale, this gazebo will be the highlight of any yard. With a cupola—topped by an elegant weathervane—a railed perimeter and a raised foundation, this plan is the essence of historic design.

Small enough to fit on just about any size lot, yet large enough to accommodate a small crowd, it is perfect for outdoor entertaining. Host a wedding, have a quartet entertain a romantic evening, or simply sit and enjoy nature as it unfolds around you. Choose standard, pre-cut gingerbread details from your local supplier or get creative with do-it-yourself designs to make it your own.

Rural Hideaway
Plan HPT160014

Features At A Glance:

- *Large Overall Area*
- *Roomy Loft*
- *Separate Work Area*

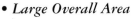

See page 124 to order complete construction drawings for this plan.

This large, sturdy lawn shed is not quite "as big as a barn," but almost! A combined area of 768 square feet includes a 24'x16' loft area with access by ladder or stairway. The structure is built entirely of standard framing materials requiring no special beams or cutting. An ideal hideaway for the serious artist, this structure could serve a myriad of other uses including a second garage, a game house, or even as a barn for small livestock.

The large tool room at the back has a built-in work bench with plenty of natural light, plus entrances from inside or outside. If your house has a fireplace, space is provided for a built-in wood stockpile area. The same space could be used to extend the length of the tool room. A 6'x7' sliding-door entrance with crossbars, and a louvered cupola accent the rural effect.

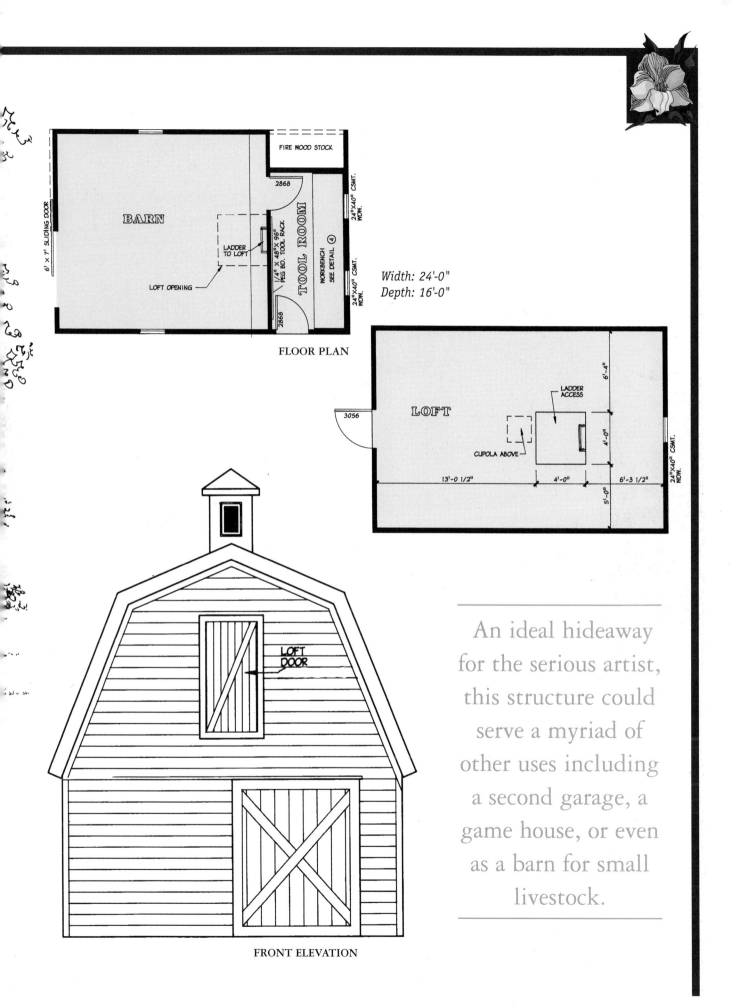

FIRE WOOD STOCK

BARN

2868

6' × 7' SLIDING DOOR

LADDER TO LOFT

LOFT OPENING

1/4" × 48" × 96" PEG BD. TOOL RACK

TOOL ROOM

WORKBENCH SEE DETAIL ④

2868

24"×40" CSMT. WDW.

24"×40" CSMT. WDW.

FLOOR PLAN

Width: 24'-0"
Depth: 16'-0"

LOFT

LADDER ACCESS

CUPOLA ABOVE

3056

6'-4"

4'-0"

13'-0 1/2"

4'-0"

6'-3 1/2"

5'-0"

24"×40" CSMT. WDW.

LOFT DOOR

FRONT ELEVATION

An ideal hideaway for the serious artist, this structure could serve a myriad of other uses including a second garage, a game house, or even as a barn for small livestock.

Barnyard Charm
Plan HPT160015

Width: 12'-0"
Depth: 8'-0"

FLOOR PLAN

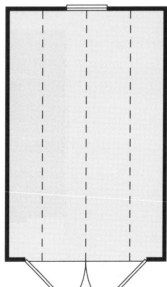

A single window at
the rear illuminates
the inside.

Features At A Glance:

- *Accommodates Large Machinery*
- *Provides Extra Storage*
- *Roomy Interior*

See page 124 to order complete construction drawings for this plan.

Barnyard charm is captured in this smaller lawn shed version. Vertical wood siding and barnyard-style double doors can accommodate large machinery comfortably. This lawn shed can also act as a home storage extension for numerous boxes, old bed frames, unused pet cages and other sundry items, which cannot be stored inside the home due to a lack of space. Workshop tools and other garden supplies can also be accommodated inside this 96-square-foot structure. A single window at the rear illuminates the inside.

Make it into a potting shed by building a set of shelves inside and out, or build in a workbench for the craftsman in the family. Flower beds may be added outside this design to decorate and blend this structure more comfortably into the home garden scene.

Quaint Countryside
Plan HPT160016

Width: 8'-0"
Depth: 12'-0"

Keep a wood stockpile dry in the winter for firewood.

FLOOR PLAN

Features At A Glance:

- *Barnyard Style*
- *Accommodating Double-doors*
- *Seasonal Efficiency*

See page 124 to order complete construction drawings for this plan.

Rustic and efficient style is plentiful and apparent is this quaint countryside design. Reflecting well upon a farmhouse scene, this barnyard shed boasts simplicity and a useful country charm. Through double doors, an expandable interior can easily house the lawn mower, yard equipment, or potting supplies for the family garden.

The 96-square-foot interior can be used differently throughout the year as seasons change. Keep a wood stockpile dry in the winter for firewood. In the spring, utilize the interior space for planting supplies. Store extra lawn chairs in the summer. And keep bagged raked leaves from blowing over in the fall.

Stylish Storage
Plan HPT160017

Features At A Glance:

- *Flexible Design*
- *Complements Many House Styles*
- *Additional Outdoor Living Area*

See page 124 to order complete construction drawings for this plan.

No words quite convey everything this generous storage shed/covered patio combination has to offer. The 120-square feet of storage area presents a delightful facade that belies its practical function. Grooved plywood siding and a shingled double roof are accented by double doors, shutters at the window, a birdhouse tucked in the eaves and a trellis for your favorite climbers. And if that's not enough, the extended roofline covers a 10'x10' patio area complete with graceful support columns and topped by a jaunty cupola.

Use the storage area as a potting or storage shed or workshop. You'll know immediately how to use the patio!

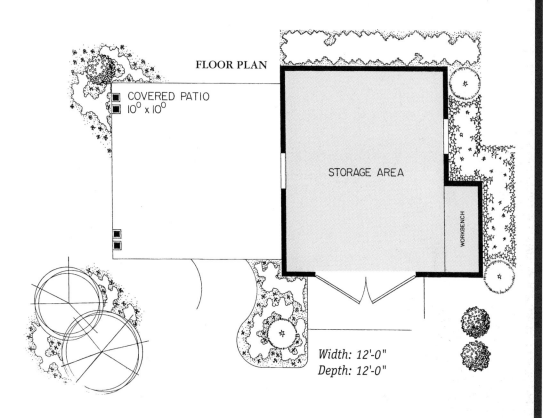

FLOOR PLAN

COVERED PATIO
10^0 x 10^0

STORAGE AREA

WORKBENCH

Width: 12'-0"
Depth: 12'-0"

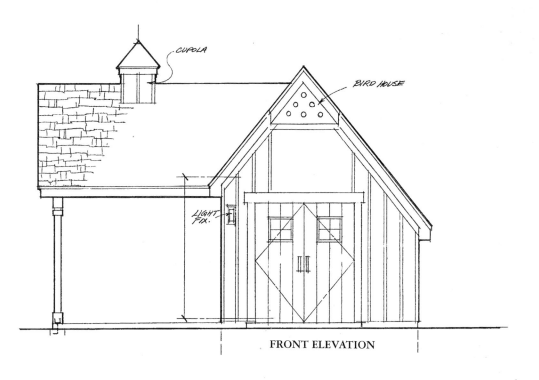

CUPOLA

BIRD HOUSE

LIGHT FIX.

FRONT ELEVATION

Rural Motif
Plan HPT160018

Width: 11'-11"
Depth: 11'-11"

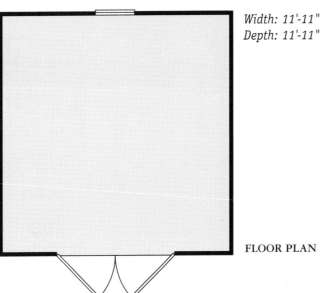

FLOOR PLAN

Features At A Glance:

- *Complements Country Settings*
- *Double-door Access*
- *Convertible Workshop*

See page 124 to order complete construction drawings for this plan.

Country living is complete with this barnyard-style shed, which complements any country or farmhouse setting as a quaint rural motif. Double doors open to accommodate and house any large lawn machinery—even a small tractor!

Inside this 144-square-foot, wood-siding structure, space can be divided for tool and wood storage, or even a small outdoor workshop area. By simply building in shelves or a work bench, this design provides a variety of uses. A window at the rear of the barn-like shed illuminates the inside for extra light, making it easier to maneuver inside during the day.

Yard Organizer
Plan HPT160019

Width: 19'-11"
Depth: 12'-0"

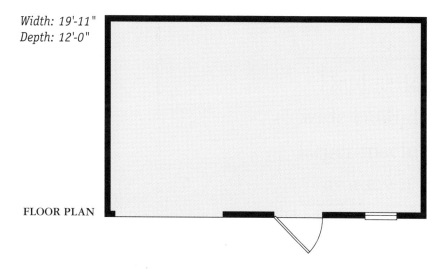

FLOOR PLAN

Features At A Glance:

- *Efficient Yard Organizer*
- *Spacious Square Footage*
- *Safe Storage Area*

See page 124 to order complete construction drawings for this plan.

This design is perfect for the efficient yard organizer. Structured with vertical wood siding and a barnyard-style door, this design thrives in any type of country setting and complements many farmhouse designs as well. Inside, a single window brightens the interior, while 240 square feet of space may be divided among a variety of different yard supplies, built-in benches or added shelving.

Gardening tools and chemicals may be stored safely and efficiently away from the home. During long winter months, extra firewood may be stacked inside the enclosed room or outside in the covered garage area. Special yard machinery and tools may be accessed and stored in a separate shed area, for convenient use.

Two-Door Tudor
Plan HPT160020

Features At A Glance:

- *Charming Window Seat*
- *Separate Storage Room*
- *Large Floor Area*

See page 124 to order complete construction drawings for this plan.

Lawn-shed extraordinaire, this appealing design can be easily converted from the Tudor style shown here, to match just about any exterior design you prefer. In addition to serving as a lawn shed, this versatile structure also can be used as a craft studio, a pool house, or a delightful playhouse for your children.

The double doors and large floor area provide ample access and storage capacity for lawn tractors and other large pieces of equipment. A handy built-in work bench offers needed space for potting plants or working on craft projects. A separate storage room for craft supplies, lawn-care products or pool chemicals can be locked for safety. Strategically placed on your site, this charming building could be designed to be a reflection of your home in miniature.

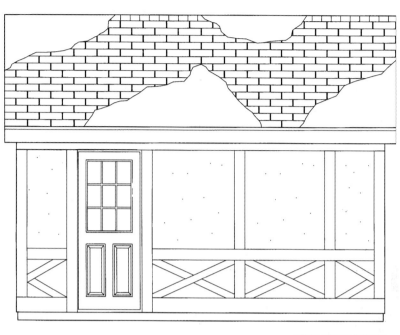

Width: 8'-0"
Depth: 16'-0"

SIDE ELEVATION

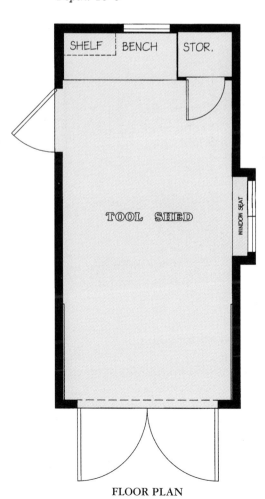

SHELF | BENCH | STOR.

TOOL SHED

WINDOW SEAT

FLOOR PLAN

The double doors and large floor area provide ample access and storage capacity for lawn tractors and other large pieces of equipment

Optimum Efficiency
Plan HPT160021

Width: 7'-11"
Depth: 8'-0"

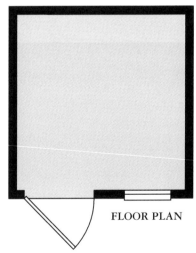

FLOOR PLAN

A versatile design, it could also easily be made into an outdoor playhouse.

Features At A Glance:

- *Petite, Yet Efficient*
- *Wood Siding*
- *Ample Storage Space*

See page 124 to order complete construction drawings for this plan.

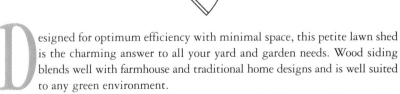

Designed for optimum efficiency with minimal space, this petite lawn shed is the charming answer to all your yard and garden needs. Wood siding blends well with farmhouse and traditional home designs and is well suited to any green environment.

Inside, 64 square feet provide ample storage space. Good for a stand-alone potting shed, or simple garden equipment storage, a window helps provide abundant light to the interior. Outside, decorative potted plants can be added to enhance the exterior. A versatile design, it could also easily be made into an outdoor playhouse.

Simple Garden Supplier
Plan HPT160022

Width: 11'-11"
Depth: 8'-0"

> A single window brightens the interior once you are through the door.

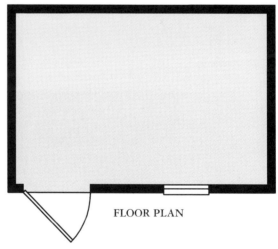

FLOOR PLAN

Features At A Glance:

- *Complements Traditional Home Exteriors*
- *Abundant Space*
- *Convertible Playhouse*

See page 124 to order complete construction drawings for this plan.

Wood siding frames the outer structure of this 96-square-foot lawn shed, which quaintly reflects most traditional home exteriors. A single window brightens the interior, and once you are through the door, notice there is plenty of space for large outdoor equipment. Not only will this structure store yard tools and garden supplies, but other recreational equipment such as bicycles, snow sleds and skies can also be accommodated. And talk about versatility!

Build this design for your kids as a playhouse, then later when they're grown and gone—Presto!—you have the perfect storage shed.

Little House In The Garden
Plan HPT160023

Features At A Glance:

- *Easy to Build*
- *Functional*
- *Multi-Use*

See page 124 to order complete construction drawings for this plan.

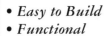

Designed to blend into the garden surroundings, this cozy little building keeps all your garden tools and supplies at your fingertips. You can vary the materials to create the appearance best suited to your site. This 72-square-foot structure is large enough to accommodate a potting bench, shelves and an area for garden tools. The window above the potting bench allows ample light, but electricity could be added easily.

Although the house is designed to be built on a concrete slab, you could use treated lumber for the floor joists, and set it right on the ground. To convert this shed design to a playhouse, simply change the window shelf into a planter and add a step with a handrail at the door.

You can vary the materials to create the appearance best suited to your site.

FRONT ELEVATION

Width: 12'-0"
Depth: 6'-0"

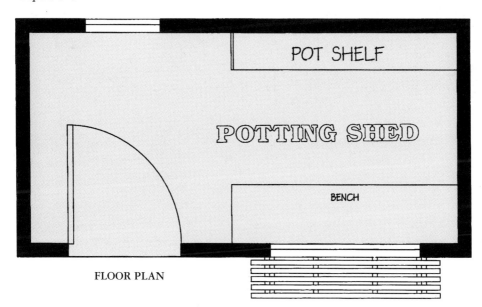

POT SHELF

POTTING SHED

BENCH

FLOOR PLAN

Abounding Space
Plan HPT160024

Width: 11'-11"
Depth: 12'-0"

FLOOR PLAN

Storage space abounds in
this simple, yet efficiently
designed lawn shed.

Features
At A Glance:

- *Abounding Space*
- *Simple Structure*
- *Well-lit Interior*

*See page 124 to order complete
construction drawings for this plan.*

See page 124 to order complete construction drawings for this plan.

Storage space abounds in this simple, yet efficiently designed lawn shed.
With the look of a petite home, this wood-siding structure is a charming
addition to any family yard.

Tools, garden supplies, outdoor equipment and even firewood can be accommodated
with extra room to spare. The interior is well-lit by a single window, and built-ins
such as benches, tool cabinets or shelves can be added to further utilize more space.

Countryside Scene
Plan HPT160025

Width: 19'-11"
Depth: 12'-0"

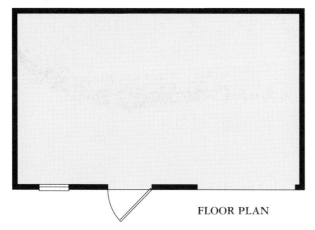

FLOOR PLAN

> A single window illuminates the enclosed portion of the plan.

Features At A Glance:

- *Enormous Square Footage*
- *Divided Space*
- *Blends Into Any Environment*

See page 124 to order complete construction drawings for this plan.

Horizontal wood siding encloses 240 square feet of storage space inside this traditional lawn-shed design. A single door and window illuminate the enclosed portion of the plan.

Space may be divided up among gardening tools, yard supplies, firewood and perhaps even a workshop area. One section of the lawn shed may be opened to offer space and convenience to larger machinery such as lawn mowers, bicycles, mopeds and scooters. This design is sure to blend into any countryside or city scene and is a great addition to the family property.

Double Duty
Plan HPT160026

Features At A Glance:

- *Dual Functions*
- *Skylight*
- *Large Storage Capacity*

See page 124 to order complete construction drawings for this plan.

Open the double doors of this multi-purpose structure and it's a mini-garage for garden tools. Enter by the single door, and it's a potting shed. The tool-shed section is large enough to house the largest lawn tractor, with room to spare for other garden equipment such as shovels, rakes, lawn trimmers and hoses.

With windows on all sides and a skylight above the potting bench, the interior has plenty of natural light; the addition of electrical wiring would make this structure even more practical. The design is shown in a Victorian style, but can be modified to match any gable-roof home design.

Open the double doors of this multi-purpose structure and it's a mini-garage for garden tools.

FRONT ELEVATION

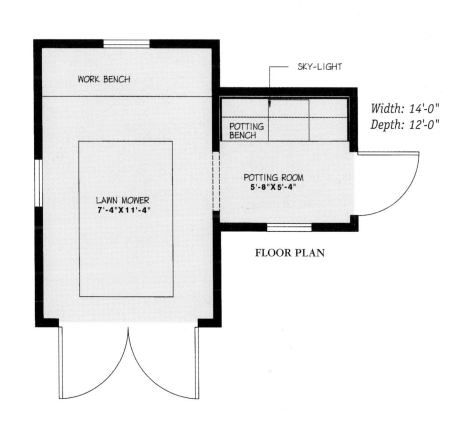

WORK BENCH

SKY-LIGHT

POTTING
BENCH

Width: 14'-0"
Depth: 12'-0"

POTTING ROOM
5'-8"X 5'-4"

LAWN MOWER
7'-4"X 11'-4"

FLOOR PLAN

A Rustic Blend
Plan HPT160027

Width: 8'-0"
Depth: 16'-0"

WORK BENCH

shed
7'-4" x 11'-4"

PORCH

FLOOR PLAN

Features At A Glance:

- *Cedar Shingles*
- *Covered Front Porch*
- *Built-in Work Bench*

See page 124 to order complete construction drawings for this plan.

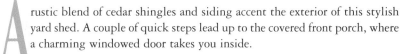

A rustic blend of cedar shingles and siding accent the exterior of this stylish yard shed. A couple of quick steps lead up to the covered front porch, where a charming windowed door takes you inside.

The interior is enhanced by a large bumped-out window, which illuminates every corner. A built-in work bench is an efficient addition to this design. The whole plan can be utilized for a private workshop, a classy potting shed or a playhouse—or make it into an extra storage space for seasonal outdoor equipment.

The Handyman's Haven

Plan HPT160028

Width: 11'-11"
Depth: 12'-0"

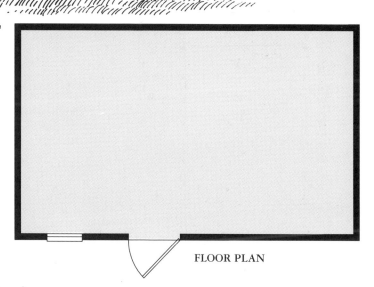

FLOOR PLAN

Features At A Glance:

- *Spacious Design*
- *Can Accommodate Large Yard Equipment*
- *Convertible Workshop*

See page 124 to order complete construction drawings for this plan.

This spacious, yet traditional lawn-shed design is ideal for both the storage of large yard equipment and as a potting shed. Traditional wood siding and a rear sloped ceiling define the well-executed exterior.

Inside, 144 square feet can be divided among yard machinery such as lawn mowers and garden tools, or used as additional storage space for homes without ample indoor storage. This structure is even large enough to accommodate a workshop—perfect for the family handyman.

"Boat"anical Beauty
Plan HPT160029

Features At A Glance:

- *Roomy Studio/Loft*
- *Ample Storage Area*
- *Lots of Natural Light*

See page 124 to order complete construction drawings for this plan.

This large multi-level garden shed can be modified easily to become a boat house if yours is a nautical family. It encompasses a generous 320 square feet, plus a convenient storage loft, and is totally contemporary in design. The built-in potting bench features removable planks to accommodate flats of flowers in various sizes. The roomy loft provides 133 square feet of safe storage area for chemicals, fertilizers or other lawn-care products.

Natural light floods the interior through multiple windows in the rear wall and in the front, across from the storage loft. This practical structure can also be used as a studio or, placed at the water's edge, it can be easily converted to a boat house by adding 4'x4' columns used as piers in lieu of the slab floor.

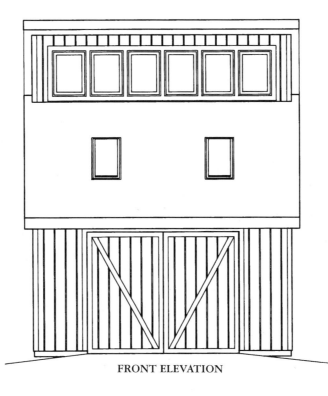

FRONT ELEVATION

The built-in
potting bench
features removable
planks to
accommodate
flats of flowers in
various sizes.

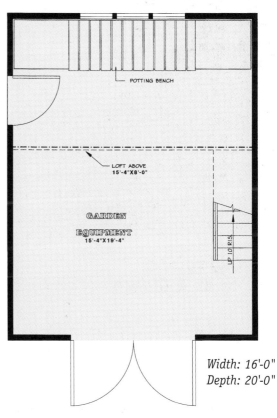

POTTING BENCH

LOFT ABOVE
15'-4"X8'-0"

GARDEN
EQUIPMENT
15'-4"X19'-4"

UP 10 RIS.

Width: 16'-0"
Depth: 20'-0"

FLOOR PLAN

Practical and Petite
Plan HPT160030

This outdoor
storage space is a
charming addition
to any rustic
environment.

Width: 8'-0"
Depth: 12'-0"

FLOOR PLAN

Features
At A Glance:

- *Narrow Design*
- *Efficiently Spaced*
  Interior
- *Barnyard-Style Door*

*See page 124 to order complete
construction drawings for this plan.*

Petite, practical and perfectly blended with any neighborhood yard, this
lawn shed is designed for style and efficiency. The outer facade is graced
with traditional wood siding and accented by a barnyard-style door.

Inside, 96 square feet expand the interior for all sorts of garden tools and yard
supplies. The sloped ceiling adds a soft finesse to the structural appearance, and
a single window brightens the interior. This outdoor storage space is a charming
addition to any rustic environment.

For The Modern Backyard
Plan HPT160031

Width: 7'-11"
Depth: 6'-0"

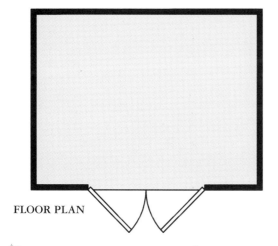

FLOOR PLAN

Double doors open
wide enough to house
larger machinery, such
as a lawn mower.

Features At A Glance:

- *Petite Yard Organizer*
- *Sloped Ceiling*
- *Wide Double Doors*

See page 124 to order complete construction drawings for this plan.

This modern-day lawn shed design is an efficient structure for any backyard scene. A wooden plank exterior encloses 48 square feet of storage space, which can be utilized in a number of various ways. Garden tools will abound in the spacious interior and firewood will be kept dry through the winter. Double doors open wide enough to house larger machinery, such as a lawn mower. The sloped ceiling enhances the modern-day exterior. A flower bed may be a quaint decorative choice to add colorful spice to the outside, while built-in shelves may be added inside to help maintain efficiency of space.

Change-Up
Plan HPT160032

Features At A Glance:

- *Versatile Design*
- *Moveable*
- *Ample Storage*

See page 124 to order complete construction drawings for this plan.

Here's a unique design that can be converted to serve a variety of functions: a tool shed, a barbecue stand, a pool-supply depot or a sports-equipment locker. Apply a little "what-if" imagination to come up with additional ways to use this versatile design to enhance your outdoor living space.

As a tool shed, this design features a large potting bench with storage above and below. Second, as a summer kitchen, it includes a built-in grill, a sink and a refrigerator. Third, for use as a pool-supply depot or equipment storage, it comes with a locker to store chemicals or valuable sports equipment safely.

This structure is designed to be movable but, depending on its function, could be placed on a concrete slab.

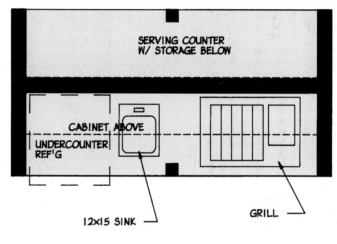

TOOL STOR.

SHELF

POTTING BENCH

Width: 8'-0"
Depth: 4'-0"

FLOOR PLAN

SERVING COUNTER
W/ STORAGE BELOW

CABINET ABOVE

UNDERCOUNTER
REF'G

12×15 SINK

GRILL

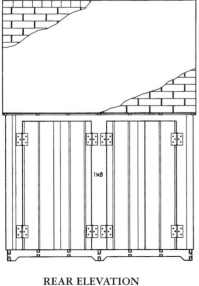

5/8" TI-II CEDAR
SIDING, GROOVE
8" O.C.

SIDE ELEVATION

1×8

REAR ELEVATION

Apply a little "what-if" imagination to come up with additional ways to use this versatile design to enhance your outdoor living space.

Three Bin Composter
Plan HPT160033

FRANK FRETZ

Efficient recycling of biodegradable kitchen scraps and garden trimmings into useful chemical-free fertilizer has never been easier with this state-of-the-art compost bin. Simply collect and toss appropriate organic materials through the hatch of the "holding" section of this three-bin unit. The covered bin helps keep the compost moist while keeping out excess moisture. With the right amount of moisture and sufficient oxygen regulated in this well-designed unit, organic matter will heat quickly and decompose thoroughly. Then transfer and "turn" the compost between the two additional side-by-side bins for continuous composting.

Resting on a sturdy base and floor, each bin holds 27 cubic feet of organic material. Removable front slats allow you to remove a few at a time—to work with an existing pile—or all at once to transfer layers for processing from one bin to the next. *Complete instructions for this useful, easy-to-build composter follow.*

PROCEDURE FOR COMPOST BINS

Base: Nail a header to each end of the center floor joist, using 16d nails. Nail the outside joists, front and back, across the ends of the headers. Nail the brace blocks in place between the joists. Locate and nail the four short floorboards across the joists where the partitions will be located, using 8d nails, as shown.

Partitions: For each of the four partitions (two outside and two inside), nail six partition boards to connect two corner posts. Nail the inside door tracks to the partition boards, 1 inch back from the front corner posts. Nail the outside door tracks flush with the front of the two interior partitions. Position the assembled partitions—

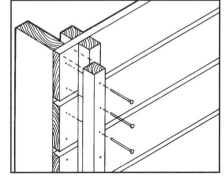

one on each end of the base and one on each side of the interior compartment; drill and bolt the corner posts to the outside joists.

Post Blocks: Cut the 2 x 6 into three pieces, to fit snugly between the bottoms of the front corner posts. Bolt the post blocks in place,

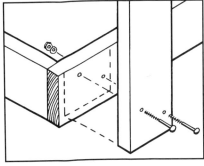

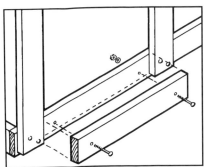

flush with the floor surface.

Floor: Nail the floor-boards in place across the joists. (There will be five for each of the two end compartments and four for the middle compartment.)

Back: Nail the back-boards in place, covering back-corner posts.

Front: Feed door slats horizontally into door tracks.

PROCEDURE

FOR LIDS

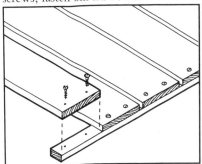

Lids: Construct two of the three lids. Using a drill and galvanized screws, fasten six lid boards to the front and back battens; allow approximately ½ inch between boards. Each lid will measure 36 inches across. Construct the third lid in the same manner, but leave out the two middle boards.

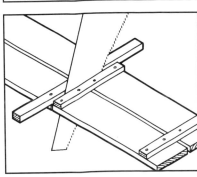

Hatch: Fasten the hatch battens to the two remaining lid boards, one batten approximately 2 inches from the end of the boards and one batten 18 inches from the same end. Fasten the header batten to the boards, 20 inches from the end, just behind the back-hatch batten. Cut between the header batten and the back-hatch batten to separate the hatch. Fasten the two remaining boards and header batten to the partially constructed lid. Hinge the hatch to the lid.

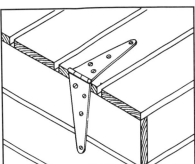

Finish: Hinge the three lids to the bins with the 3-inch hinges, so

that they are centered over the compartments. Attach a chain to the bottom of both end lids, at about the middle of the end boards, with screw eyes. Attach a chain to the bottom of both middle-lid end boards, as shown. Mount snap hooks on the ends of the chains. Use pliers to attach screw eyes to the bin partitions, as shown.

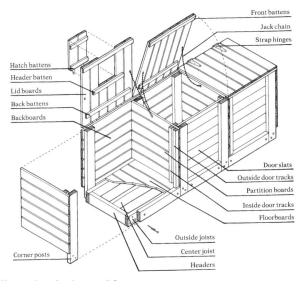

Illustrations by Carson Ode

MATERIALS FOR BINS

L U M B E R *
1 pc. 2 x 6 x 108" (center joist)
2 pcs. 2 x 6 x 30" (headers)
2 pcs. 2 x 6 x 111" (outside joists)
2 pcs. 2 x 6 x 14¼" (brace blocks)
4 pcs. 1 x 6 x 33" (short floorboards)
8 pcs. 2 x 6 x 41½" (corner posts)
24 pcs. 1 x 6 x 36" (partition boards)
6 pcs. 2 x 2 x 34" (inside door tracks)
2 pcs. 2 x 2 x 35½" (outside door-tracks)

1 pc. 2 x 6 x 96" (cut to fit for post blocks)
14 pcs. 2 x 6 x 34½" (floorboards)
6 pcs. 1 x 6 x 111" (backboards)
18 pcs. 1 x 6 x 35½" (door slats)
3 pcs. 1 x 3 x 35½" (door slats)
H A R D W A R E
22 carriage bolts ¼ x 3½" with nuts and washers
1 box galvanized nails 16d
1 box galvanized nails 8d

MATERIALS FOR LIDS

L U M B E R *
18 pcs. 1 x 6 x 37" (lid boards)
3 pcs. 1 x 2 x 36" (front battens)
3 pcs. 1 x 2 x 34" (back battens)
2 pcs. 1 x 2 x 11¼" (hatch battens)
1 pc. 1 x 2 x 22" (header batten)
H A R D W A R E
6 strap hinges 8" (lids)
2 strap hinges 4" (hatch)

4 lengths jack chain, approx. 36" each
8 heavy screw eyes
4 snap hooks
1 box galvanized screws #6 x 1¼"
T O O L S
Electric drill
Saw (jigsaw or handsaw)
Hammer
Pliers

*Editor's Note: If you prefer, use untreated pine rather than pressure-treated lumber. Paint with a low-toxicity preservative, such as copper naphthenate.

Practical and Playful
Plan HPT160037

Width: 16'-0"
Depth: 12'-0"

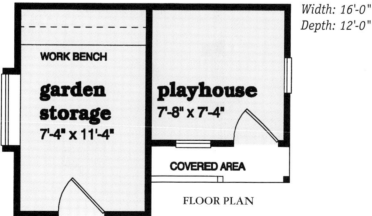

WORK BENCH

garden storage
7'-4" x 11'-4"

playhouse
7'-8" x 7'-4"

COVERED AREA

FLOOR PLAN

Features At A Glance:

- *Lawn Shed/Playhouse Combo*
- *Cedar Shingles and Siding*
- *Country Cottage Style*

See page 124 to order complete construction drawings for this plan.

See page 124 to order complete construction drawings for this plan.

Efficient for Mom and Dad, while munchkin-sized to accomodate little people—this structure boasts practicality and playfulness. The exterior is dazzled in wood siding and cedar shingles—a pleasant display for any outdoor scenery. The garden storage area is separated from the playhouse and features an efficient work bench and an illuminating side window.

The playhouse resembles a petite version of a country cottage. A tiny covered porch with a wood railing and a window accent the outside and welcome young ones into the cozy hideaway. Inside, another window graces the right wall and brightens the interior. There is room enough for a small table and chairs and, most importantly, plenty of toys.

Storybook Cottage
Plan HPT160038

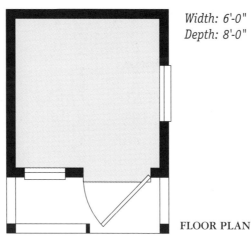

Width: 6'-0"
Depth: 8'-0"

FLOOR PLAN

Features At A Glance:

- *Make-Believe Cottage*
- *Roomy Space*
- *Petite Covered Porch*

See page 124 to order complete construction drawings for this plan.

This playhouse paradise is an outdoor haven for any youngster looking for self-made entertainment. It's a place your kids can call thier own. Similar to a storybook cottage, make-belief games will become a reality.

From the quaint covered porch with a wood railing and square supports, go inside to where this clubhouse is brightly illuminated by two windows. This roomy space can be filled with toy furniture, games, arts and crafts or anything to entertain on a rainy day.

Designer Playhouse
Plan HPT160039

Features At A Glance:

- *Mini-House Design*
- *Lots of Natural Light*
- *Loft, Ladder and Trap Door!*

See page 124 to order complete construction drawings for this plan.

This whimsical, scaled-down version of a full-sized house makes a dream-come-true playhouse for kids. Designed by Conni Cross, it features a wraparound front porch with a trellis roof, a "real" front door and a loft that can only be reached by a ladder through a trap door! Generous dimensions provide plenty of space for a 7'-4"x9'-4" play room and a 5'-8"x6'-4" bunk room. A 7'-4"x5'-4" loft overlooks the main play area.

Natural light floods all areas of this delightful play center through windows in the play room, bunk room and loft. A sturdy railing borders the loft, and built-in bunk beds in the bunk room are ready and waiting for sleepovers.

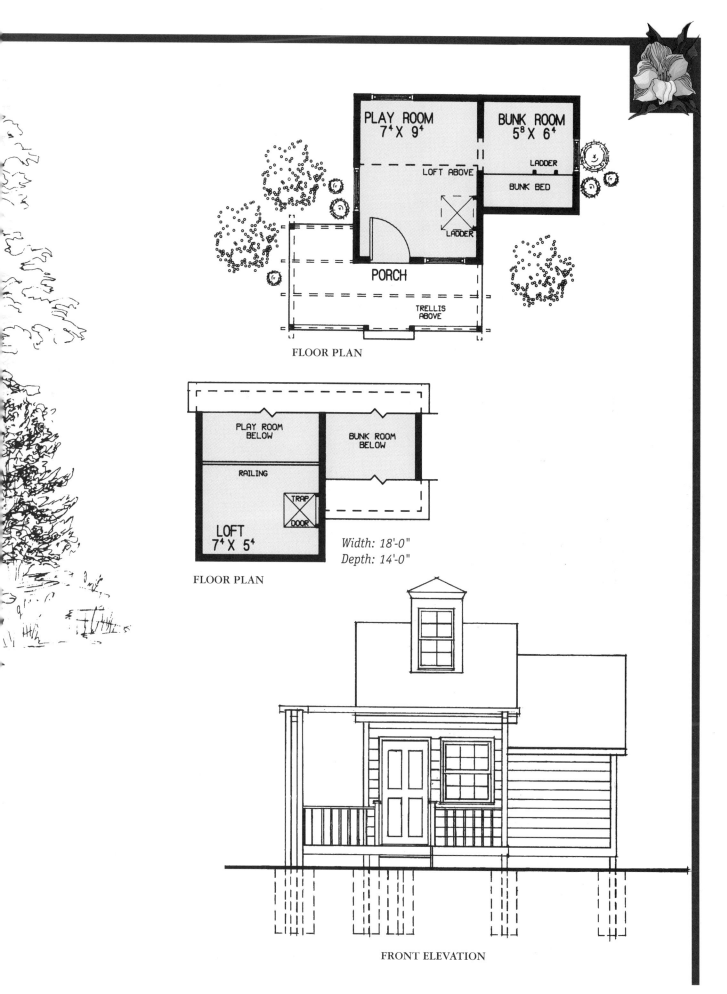

PLAY ROOM
7⁴X 9⁴

BUNK ROOM
5⁸X 6⁴

LADDER

LOFT ABOVE

BUNK BED

LADDER

PORCH

TRELLIS ABOVE

FLOOR PLAN

PLAY ROOM BELOW

BUNK ROOM BELOW

RAILING

TRAP DOOR

LOFT
7⁴X 5⁴

Width: 18'-0"
Depth: 14'-0"

FLOOR PLAN

FRONT ELEVATION

Work and/or Play
Plan HPT160040

Features At A Glance:

- *Dual-Level Roofline*
- *Easy to Build*
- *2-in-1 Use*

See page 124 to order complete construction drawings for this plan.

The kids will love this one! This functional, practical lawn shed doubles in design and capacity as a delightful playhouse complete with a covered porch, lathe-turned columns and a window box for young gardeners. The higher roofline on the shed gives the structure a two-story effect, while the playhouse design gives the simple lawn shed a much more appealing appearance. Access to the shed is through double doors. The playhouse features a single-door entrance from the porch and three bright windows.

The interior wall between the shed and playhouse could be moved another two-and-a-half feet back to make it larger. Or, remove the interior wall completely to use the entire 128-square-foot area exclusively for either the lawn shed or playhouse. The open eaves and porch columns give the structure a country appearance; however, by boxing in the eaves and modifying the columns, you can create just about any style you or the kids like best.

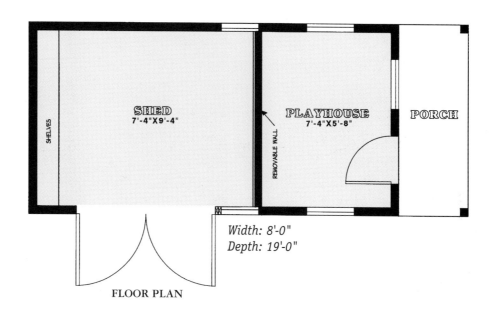

SHELVES	SHED 7'-4"X9'-4"	PLAYHOUSE 7'-4"X5'-8"	PORCH

REMOVABLE WALL

Width: 8'-0"
Depth: 19'-0"

FLOOR PLAN

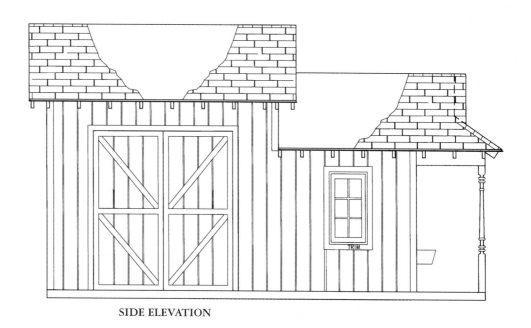

TRIM

SIDE ELEVATION

Cannot Go Wrong
Plan HPT160041

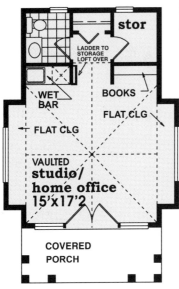

Width: 20'-0"
Depth: 30'-0"

stor

LADDER TO STORAGE LOFT OVER

WET BAR

BOOKS

FLAT CLG

← **FLAT CLG**

VAULTED studio/ home office 15'x17'2

COVERED PORCH

FLOOR PLAN

You can't go wrong by choosing the plans for this cleverly designed structure.

Features At A Glance:

• *Home Office/Studio*
• *French Door Access*
• *Loft Above Bathroom and Storage*

See page 124 to order complete construction drawings for this plan.

N eed a quiet place for a home office or studio? You can't go wrong by choosing the plans for this cleverly designed structure. It is filled with amenities that make a small space seem huge.

French doors open to an efficient and attractive layout. The ceiling of the main part of the building is vaulted and features clerestory windows to provide ample lighting. Bumped-out areas on both sides are perfect for desks and work areas. A built-in bookshelf along one wall is complemented by a large walk-in storage closet. More storage is available in the loft overhead, reachable by a ladder nearby. A half-bath and wet bar round out the plan. The entry is graced by a columned porch and double French doors flanked by fixed windows.

Weekend Cottage
Plan HPT160042

Width: 12'-0"
Depth: 16'-0"

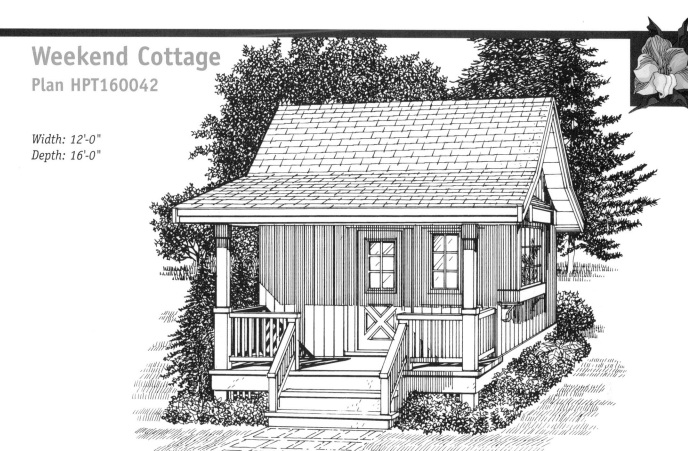

Alternate Elevation

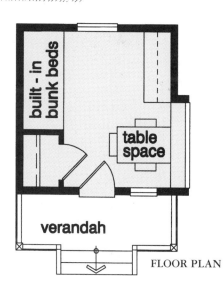

built-in bunk beds

table space

verandah

FLOOR PLAN

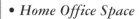

Features At A Glance:

- *Home Office Space*
- *Convertible Guest House*
- *Multiple Built-ins*

See page 124 to order complete construction drawings for this plan.

For a bare-essentials outdoor structure, this weekend cottage offers a wealth of options for its use. Choose it for handy home office space, craft cottage space, extra room for visitors, a playhouse for the kids or a game room. It features a covered front porch and offers two lovely exteriors for you to choose from—go for simple and straightforward rustic, or add a touch of romance with a Victorian look.

The interior contains built-in bunk beds, a closet, built-in shelves and a bumped-out window that works well for table space. Plans include details for both a crawlspace and slab foundation.

Sunny Craft Cottage
Plan HPT160043

Features At A Glance:

- *Lots of Windows*
- *Vaulted Ceilings*
- *Well-Designed Work Space*

See page 124 to order complete construction drawings for this plan.

The ultimate luxury for any craft enthusiast—a separate, free-standing building dedicated to your craft of choice! Functional as well as a beautiful addition to your landscape, this 250-square-foot cottage provides ample counter space and shelving to spread out or store all your materials and tools. And at break time, relax from your hobby in the attached sun room with a vaulted ceiling, French doors and lots of elegant windows.

Orient the structure on your property to face south for the sun room and the north-facing work area receives soft, even light. A built-in and well-thought-out work table is flanked by additional countertop work space. Outside, an open 10'x12' deck off the sun room makes this little cottage just about perfect.

Width: 20'-0"
Depth: 16'-0"

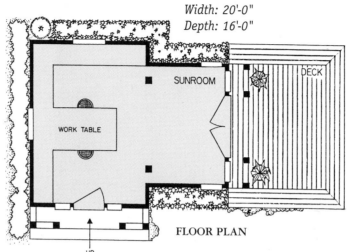

SUNROOM

DECK

WORK TABLE

FLOOR PLAN

UP

A built-in and well-thought-out
work table is flanked by additional
countertop work space.

INTERIOR

Simple in Design
Plan HPT160044

Features At A Glance:

- *Vaulted Studio*
- *Fanciful Cupola*
- *French-door Access*

See page 124 to order complete construction drawings for this plan.

Though simple in design, this smaller studio/home office provides all the right stuff for your work space. A fanciful cupola, two octagonal windows and detailed stickwork combine to give this basic little design a touch of class. A covered entry shelters the double French-door access to a two-room area. The smaller space features a nine-foot flat ceiling and is separated from the main studio area by a columned arch. The main area seems larger than it is thanks to a vaulted ceiling and two bumped-out windows.

Define your own work area with furniture, or modify this design to include handy built-ins.

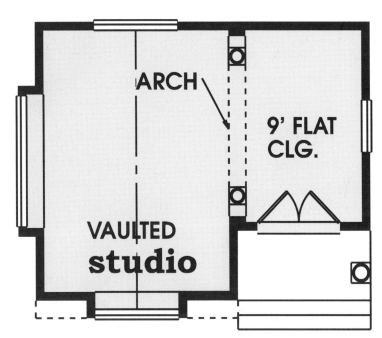

Width: 20'-0"
Depth: 16'-0"

ARCH

9' FLAT CLG.

VAULTED
studio

FLOOR PLAN

Define your own work area with
furniture, or modify this design to
include handy built-ins.

Town and Country
Plan HPT160045

Features At A Glance:

- *Uses All Utilities*
- *Large Kitchen Area*
- *Half Bath*

See page 124 to order complete construction drawings for this plan.

This versatile design features a unique siding pattern: a little bit of country with a pinch of contemporary sophistication. You can build this 428-square-foot, multi-purpose structure on a slab or crawlspace or even with a basement! Planned to take advantage of natural light from all sides, this design will make a perfect studio, game room or office. Or, add a shower in the lavatory room and it becomes a guest house.

Features include a half-bath, a 6' x 8' kitchen—large enough for a stove and refrigerator—and a utility room with ample space for a furnace and hot-water tank. With all the amenities provided, you could work or relax here for days without ever leaving! The front porch area is a charming place to relax and put your feet up as you or your guests contemplate the events of the day.

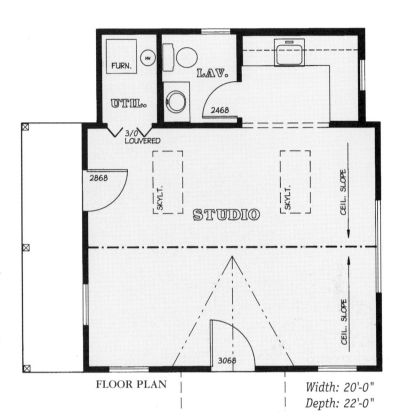

FLOOR PLAN

Width: 20'-0"
Depth: 22'-0"

FURN.

LAV.

UTIL.

3/0
LOUVERED

2868

2468

SKYLT.

SKYLT.

STUDIO

CEIL. SLOPE

CEIL. SLOPE

3068

With all the amenities provided, you could work or relax here for days without ever leaving!

FRONT ELEVATION

Excellent Exercise Cottage
Plan HPT160046

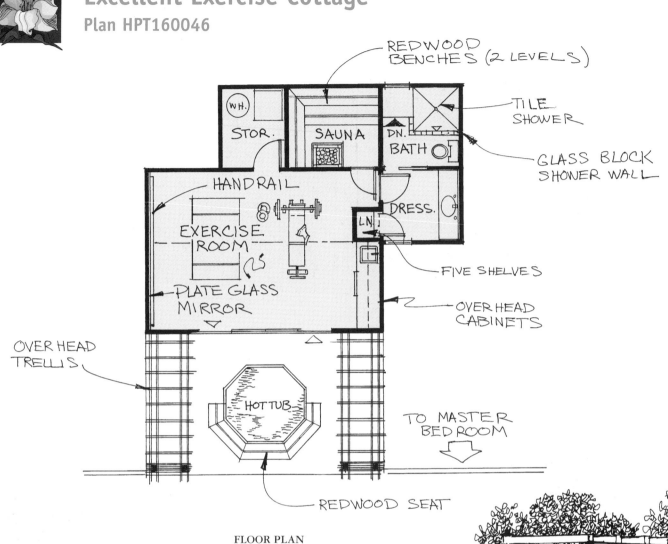

REDWOOD
BENCHES (2 LEVELS)

TILE
SHOWER

GLASS BLOCK
SHOWER WALL

W.H.

STOR.

SAUNA

DN.

BATH

HANDRAIL

DRESS.

LN.

EXERCISE
ROOM

FIVE SHELVES

PLATE GLASS
MIRROR

OVER HEAD
CABINETS

OVER HEAD
TRELLIS

HOT TUB

TO MASTER
BEDROOM

REDWOOD SEAT

FLOOR PLAN

Features At A Glance:

- *Vaulted Ceiling*
- *Sauna and Hot Tub*
- *Half-Bath and Mini-Kitchen*

See page 124 to order complete construction drawings for this plan.

If you're serious about maintaining optimum personal fitness, don't turn the page until you check out this free-standing exercise cottage. A wall of mirrors, double-decked windows and sliding doors, vaulted ceilings, plus 250 square feet of floor space provide all the room you need for your workouts and much, much more. High ceilings accommodate the largest equipment, and features include plenty of storage, a mini-kitchen and bathroom facilities with a glass-block shower wall. Add a sauna inside, and a hot tub outside, and who could ask for anything more?

A ballet bar against the mirrored wall, two-level redwood benches in the sauna and ample storage shelves and cabinets are additional amenities in this inviting personal gym.

INTERIOR

A separate dressing room and linen closet
are also included in this design.

Teen Territory
Plan HPT160047

Features At A Glance:

- *Lots of Space*
- *Vaulted Ceiling*
- *Free-Standing Design*

See page 124 to order complete construction drawings for this plan.

Lucky are the teenagers who have the option of staking claim to this private retreat! The overall dimensions of 16'x22' provide plenty of space for study, TV or just hangin' out. Special features include a raised, carpeted platform in the TV lounge; a comfy window seat for reading or a catnap; a separate niche for electronic games; and a unique, brightly painted graffiti wall in the entryway.

Wired for sound, bright colors and windows in a variety of shapes mark this specially designed, free-standing building as teens-only territory.

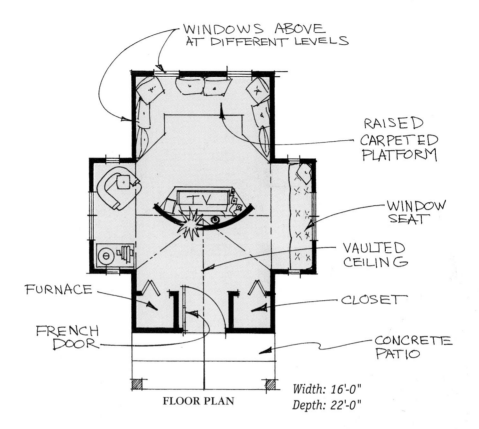

WINDOWS ABOVE
AT DIFFERENT LEVELS

RAISED
CARPETED
PLATFORM

WINDOW
SEAT

VAULTED
CEILING

TV

FURNACE

CLOSET

FRENCH
DOOR

CONCRETE
PATIO

FLOOR PLAN

Width: 16'-0"
Depth: 22'-0"

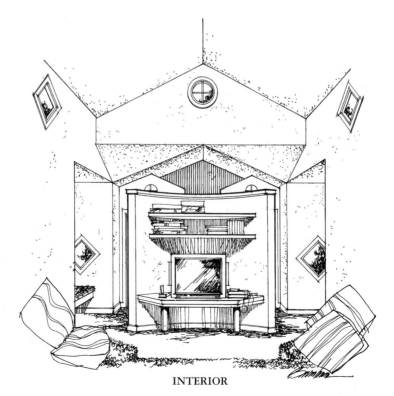

INTERIOR

Camelot
Plan HPT160048

Features At A Glance:

- *Innovative Design*
- *Uses Standard Materials*
- *For Kids of All Ages*

See page 124 to order complete construction drawings for this plan.

Lords and ladies, knights and evil-doers—this playhouse has everything except a fire-breathing dragon! Your children will spend hours re-enacting the days of Kings and Queens and Knights of the Round Table.

Surprisingly easy to build, this playset right out of King Arthur's Court uses standard materials. One corner of the playhouse holds a 4'x4' sandbox. A stairway leads to a 3'x3' tower with its own catwalk. The area under the stairway could be enclosed to make a storage room for toys...or a dungeon to hold the captured Black Knight. The double castle doors can be fitted with standard hardware, but wrought-iron hinges will make this innovative playhouse look even more like a castle.

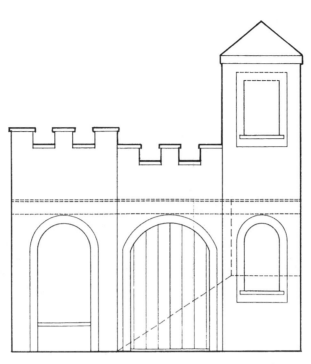

FRONT ELEVATION

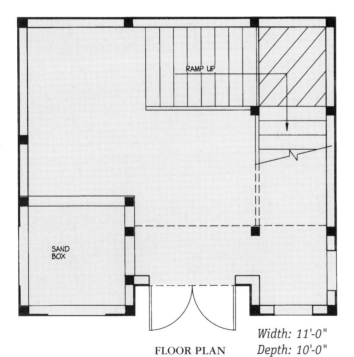

RAMP UP

SAND BOX

FLOOR PLAN

Width: 11'-0"
Depth: 10'-0"

Your children
will spend hours
re-enacting the
days of Kings and
Queens and
Knights of the
Round Table.

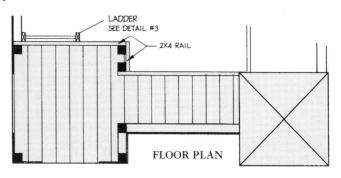

LADDER
SEE DETAIL #3

2X4 RAIL

FLOOR PLAN

Swings and Things
Plan HPT160049

Features At A Glance:

- *Easy to Build*
- *Designed for Lots of Use*
- *Versatile*

See page 124 to order complete construction drawings for this plan.

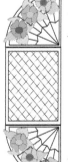

A playset with a little bit of everything. The Swings: This playset is designed to use any of the shelf-style swing units available at your local supplier. The Slides: There are two slides: One regular; the other an enclosed spiral slide to provide added thrills. The Ramp: The ramp is designed for kids who like to climb back up the slide. Now they can climb up the ramp and slide down the slide on the other side. For small children, you can add a knotted rope to help them up. The Eagle's Nest: The climb to the Eagle's Nest will provide your kids with exercise for their muscles and their imagination. Young children will love to switch from one part of this playset to another, over and over again.

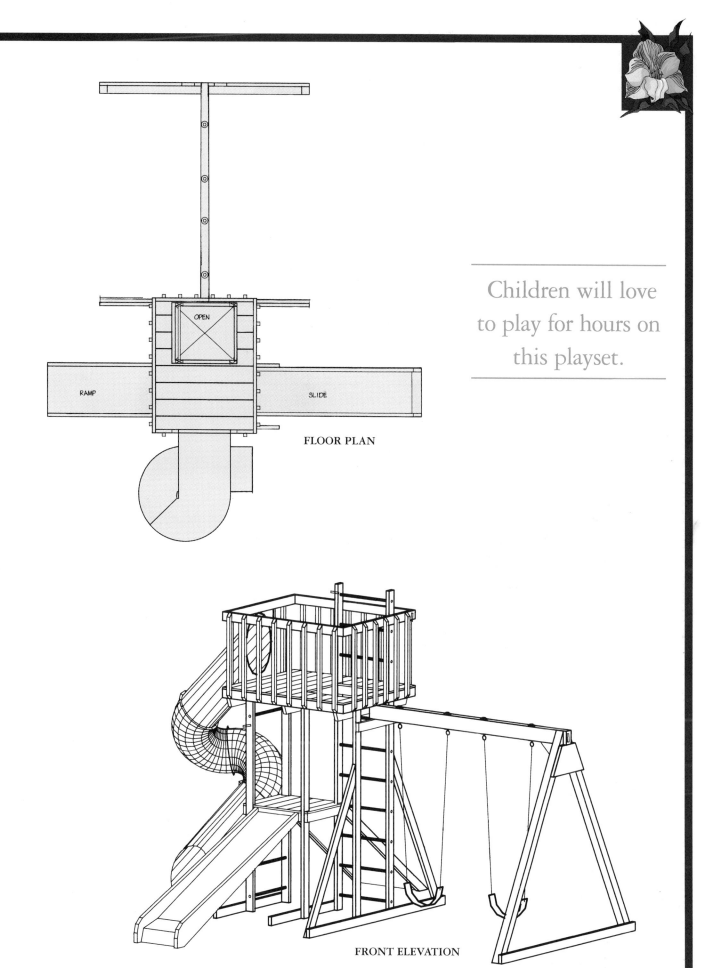

OPEN

RAMP

SLIDE

FLOOR PLAN

Children will love
to play for hours on
this playset.

FRONT ELEVATION

Swinging Bridge
Plan HPT160050

Features At A Glance:

- *Variety of Equipment*
- *Easy to Build*
- *Sturdy*

See page 124 to order complete construction drawings for this plan.

The highlight of this delightful playset is the swinging bridge. It is available ready-made in a variety of styles or you can make it yourself. Either way, be sure to check that the handrail is high enough to prevent small children from toppling over the top or falling through the sides.

Designed for kids five and older, this playset includes a ladder inset at an angle to help developmental coordination. Both shelf-style swings and a popular tire swing are provided for variety. Hardware for the swings is available from your local suppliers. For larger tire swings, simply extend the support beam to accept a larger swing area. This playset is designed to sit on the ground; however, the firefighter's pole should be sunk into the ground six to eight inches to give it additional stability.

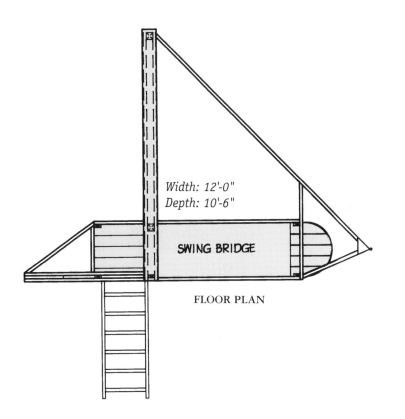

Width: 12'-0"
Depth: 10'-6"

SWING BRIDGE

FLOOR PLAN

The highlight of
this delightful
playset is the
swinging bridge.

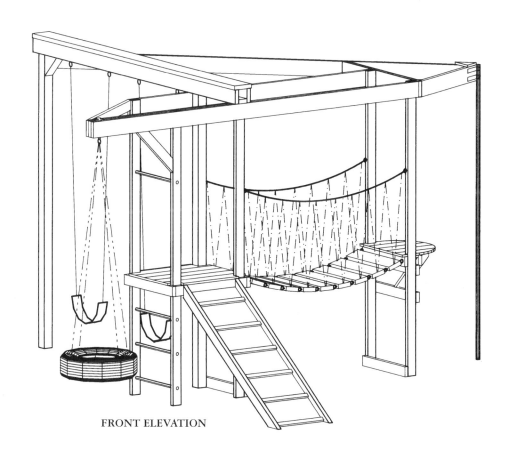

FRONT ELEVATION

The Lookout
Plan HPT160051

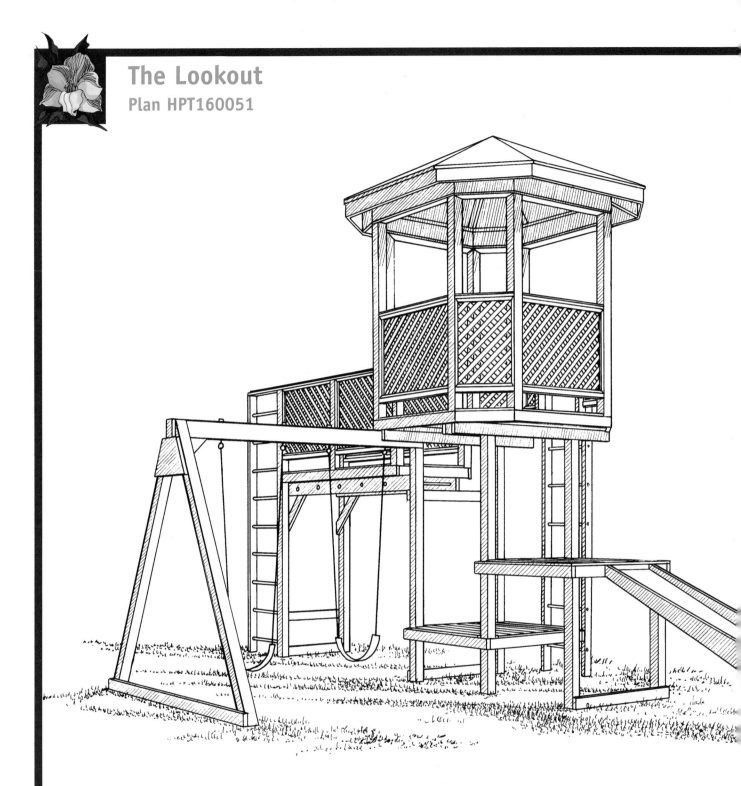

Features At A Glance:

- *Adjustable Equipment*
- *Easy to Build*
- *Versatile*

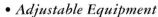

See page 124 to order complete construction drawings for this plan.

A playhouse, a tree house, a lookout tower...your children will invent many uses for this mini-gazebo perched almost eight feet above the ground. It's large enough for a small table and chairs, for a picnic or a Mad Hatter's tea party. Or, spread out some sleeping bags and invite friends for an overnight adventure—but no sleepwalking! The ladder, swings and slide all add to the fun and can be modified to accommodate the ages of your children.

If you have a full-size gazebo on your site, or plan to build one, you could use a similar design in the railings for both units for a surprising "double-take" effect.

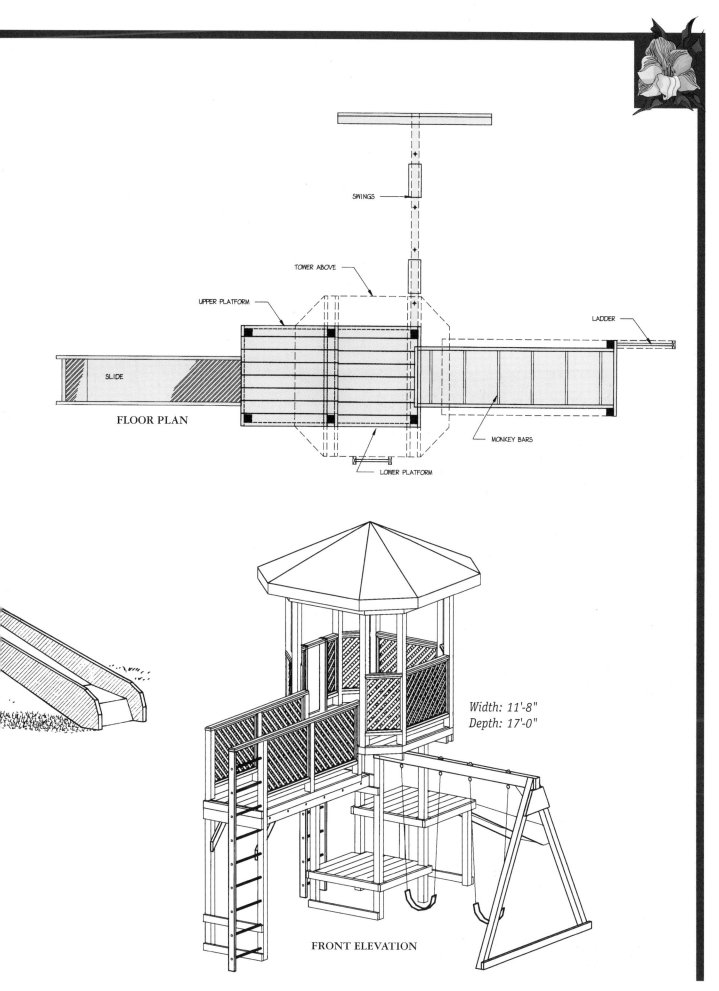

SWINGS

TOWER ABOVE

UPPER PLATFORM

LADDER

SLIDE

FLOOR PLAN

MONKEY BARS

LOWER PLATFORM

Width: 11'-8"
Depth: 17'-0"

FRONT ELEVATION

Quick Change Architecture
Plan HPT160052

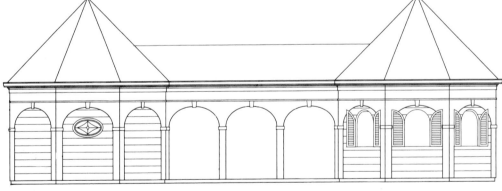

FRONT ELEVATION

Features At A Glance:

- *Optional Uses*
- *Covered Walkway*
- *Impressive Design*

See page 124 to order complete construction drawings for this plan.

The magic of this design is its flexibility. Use it exclusively as a changing cabana with separate His and Hers changing rooms, or, with a little sleight of hand, turn one of the rooms into a summer kitchen for outdoor entertaining.

As changing rooms, each eight-sided area includes built-in benches and private bathroom facilities. The 15'-3½"x 15'-3½" kitchen option includes a stove, refrigerator, food-preparation area and a storage pantry. A shuttered window poolside provides easy access to serve your guests across the counter. A covered walkway links these two areas and serves as a shaded picnic area, or a convenient place to get out of the sun. Columns, arches and stained-glass windows provide a touch of grandeur to this fun and functional poolside design.

A covered walkway
links these two
areas and serves as a
shaded picnic area,
or a convenient
place to get out
of the sun.

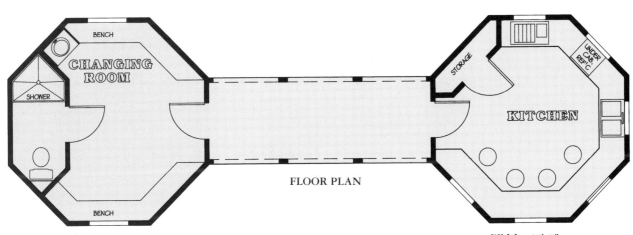

FLOOR PLAN

Width: 47'-7"
Depth: 15'-4"

Triple Duty
Plan HPT160053

Features At A Glance:

- *Lots of Built-ins*
- *Compact Size*
- *Elegant Lines*

See page 124 to order complete construction drawings for this plan.

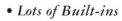

A changing room, a summer kitchen, and an elegant porch for shade. Add the convenience of bathroom facilities and you're set for outdoor living all summer long. This pool pavilion is designed to provide maximum function in a small area and features built-in benches, shelves, hanging rods and a separate linen closet for towels.

The opaque diamond-patterned windows decorate the exterior of the 10'x6'8" changing area and the mirror-image bath. The bath could also be made into a kitchen area, then simply add a sliding window to allow easy passage of refreshments to your family and guests at poolside. When you've had enough sun or socializing, recline in the shade under the columned porch and enjoy a good book or a nap.

When you've had enough sun or socializing, recline in the shade under the columned porch and enjoy a good book or a nap.

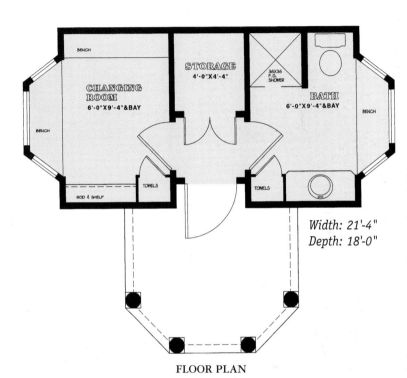

BENCH

CHANGING ROOM
6'-0"X9'-4"&BAY

STORAGE
4'-0"X4'-4"

36X36
F.G.
SHOWER

BATH
6'-0"X9'-4"&BAY

BENCH

BENCH

TOWELS

TOWELS

ROD & SHELF

Width: 21'-4"
Depth: 18'-0"

FLOOR PLAN

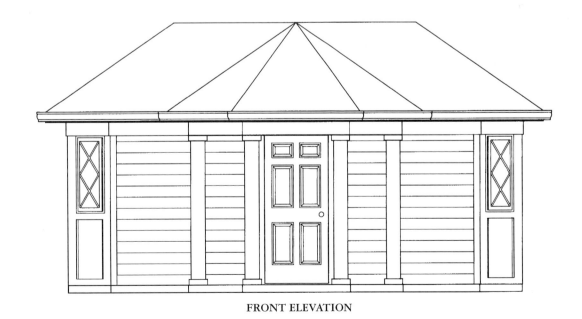

FRONT ELEVATION

Cabana Cottage
Plan HPT160054

Width: 12'-0"
Depth: 10'-0"

TOWELS

BENCH

FLOOR PLAN

PLANTER BOX

Two windows naturally
brighten the interior.

Features At A Glance:

- *Cottage Style*
- *Convenient Bathroom*
- *Towel Closet*

*See page 124 to order complete
construction drawings for this plan.*

This poolside cabana design possesses a cottage quaintness that will charm any scene. The wood siding and shingle exterior is enhanced by ornamental planter boxes—adding bright flowers to decorate your relaxing summer retreat. Two windows naturally brighten the interior. The right side houses a changing room, which features a built-in wood bench and a convenient towel closet. The left room offers an outdoor bathroom, complete with a sink, toilet and shower. Practical and comfortable, this cabana easily provides for every poolside need.

Poolside Manor
Plan HPT160055

This room is brightened by a window and features a sink, toilet, and shower for convenient use.

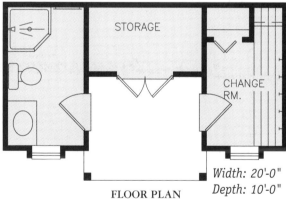

STORAGE

CHANGE RM.

FLOOR PLAN

Width: 20'-0"
Depth: 10'-0"

Features At A Glance:

- *Cedar Shingles and Siding Exterior*
- *Covered Front Porch*
- *Convenient Storage Room*

See page 124 to order complete construction drawings for this plan.

This cabana dream complements any poolside manor. A rustic blend of siding and cedar shingles graces the exterior and adds a stylish ornamentation to any private yard.

A shaded, quaint covered porch welcomes you through three separate doors. To the right, a private changing chamber offers a bench and linen closet, and is illuminated by a single window. The center room provides a separate outdoor storage area—useful for large or bulky pool equipment such at rafts, games, or tubes. To the left, a private outdoor bathroom is a useful addition. This room is brightened by a window and features a sink, toilet, and shower for convenient use. This design can save dozens of trips in and out of the home.

Rain or Shine Pool Cabana
Plan HPT160056

Features At A Glance:

- *Multi-Purpose*
- *Large Covered Area*
- *Lovely Exterior*

See page 124 to order complete construction drawings for this plan.

A mini-kitchen and an optional built-in table are tucked in the breezeway of this double room; you'll have shelter for poolside repasts no matter what the weather. You can enhance both the beauty and the function of any pool area with this charming structure. The exterior features include a gable roof with columns in the front, shuttered windows, horizontal wood and shingle siding, decorative flower boxes and a cupola.

The two rooms on either side of the breezeway area provide a 5'-8"x7'-6" changing area with built-in seating and a larger area—7'-6"x7'-6"—for convenient storage of pool supplies and equipment. This spacious cabana is sure to be a fine addition to an active family's pool area.

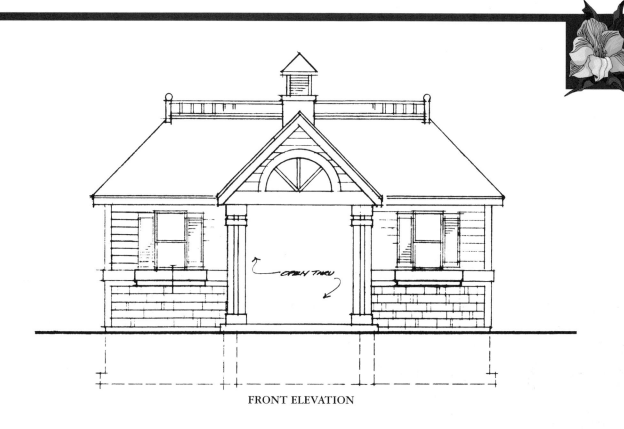

FRONT ELEVATION

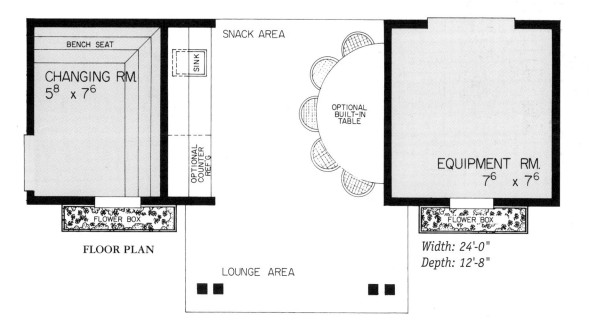

SNACK AREA

BENCH SEAT

CHANGING RM.
5⁸ x 7⁶

SINK

OPTIONAL
COUNTER
REF'G

OPTIONAL
BUILT-IN
TABLE

EQUIPMENT RM.
7⁶ x 7⁶

FLOWER BOX

FLOWER BOX

FLOOR PLAN

Width: 24'-0"
Depth: 12'-8"

LOUNGE AREA

You can enhance both the beauty and
the function of any pool area with this
charming structure.

Y'all Come!
Plan HPT160057

Features At A Glance:

- *Outdoor Kitchen*
- *Plenty of Built-ins*
- *Large Screened Room*

See page 124 to order complete construction drawings for this plan.

An outdoor kitchen and much, much more! For year-round, daylight-to-dark entertaining, consider this large outdoor entertainment unit. Nearly 700 square feet of floor space includes a deck for sunbathing by day or dancing under the stars after sundown. A 13'x 13'-2" screened room provides a pest-free environment for cards or conversation. And, the Cookout Chef will rule with a flair over a full-service kitchen area that may include a grill, wet bar, sink, refrigerator and ample room for storage.

You can locate this versatile structure adjacent to your pool, or place it as a free-standing unit wherever your landscape and site plan allow. Select material for the railings and privacy screens in patterns to match or complement your home.

Width: 26'-1"
Depth: 30'-4"

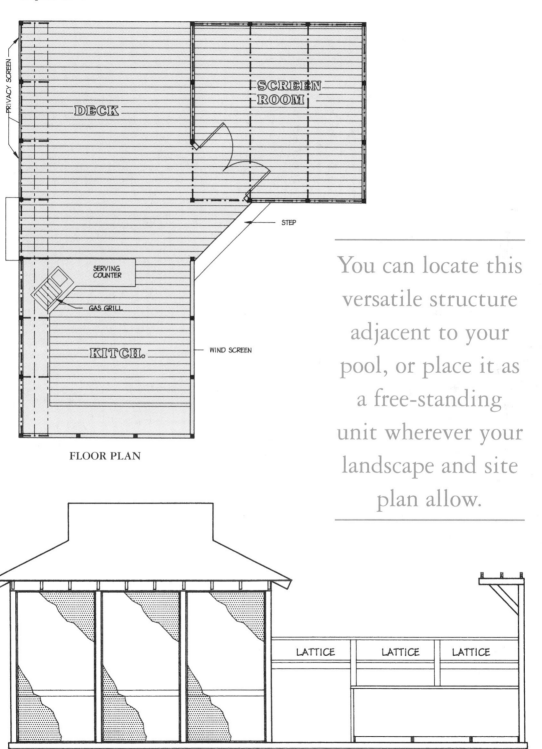

PRIVACY SCREEN

DECK

SCREEN ROOM

STEP

SERVING COUNTER

GAS GRILL

KITCH.

WIND SCREEN

FLOOR PLAN

You can locate this versatile structure adjacent to your pool, or place it as a free-standing unit wherever your landscape and site plan allow.

LATTICE   LATTICE   LATTICE

REAR ELEVATION

Barbecue Pavilion
Plan HPT160058

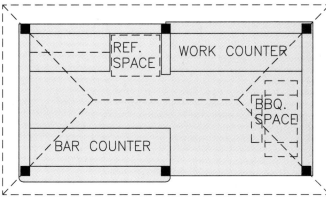

FLOOR PLAN

REF. SPACE

WORK COUNTER

BBQ. SPACE

BAR COUNTER

Width: 16'-0"
Depth: 8'-0"

Features At A Glance:
- *Convenient Barbecue Area*
- *Useful Outdoor Refrigerator*
- *A Bar Counter For Entertaining*

See page 124 to order complete construction drawings for this plan.

This stylish pavilion is an amazing outdoor retreat for any family. A hipped roof shades the inner area—keep a picnic table close by for outdoor barbecues and entertaining. To the right, a barbecue area is provided for outdoor grilling next to a convenient work counter—useful for preparing outdoor meals. A refrigerator space is also provided, next to another counter, for keeping cool foods fresh. The pavilion is completed by a bar counter, large enough to host a wide variety of refreshments.

Decorate the outer perimeters with garden-side plants. Built for the family that excels in entertaining, this structure is a lively addition to any property.

Petite Pavilion
Plan HPT160059

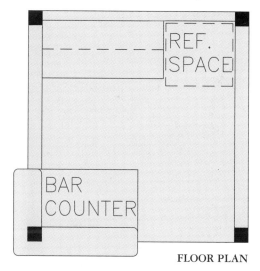

Width: 8'-0"
Depth: 8'-0"

REF. SPACE

BAR COUNTER

FLOOR PLAN

Features At A Glance:

- *Petite Design*
- *Perfect For The Poolside*
- *Built-in Shelves*

See page 124 to order complete construction drawings for this plan.

This petite pavilion design is perfect for plenty of entertaining. Build this structure close to a pool area and you could save a ton of trips in and out of the home kitchen. Summer leisure time can be more comfortably spent with this convenience close by at hand. A refrigerator space is generously provided alongside a counter preparation area. Above, built-in shelves may be added for extra storage. On the opposite side, a bar counter resides for accessible convenience.

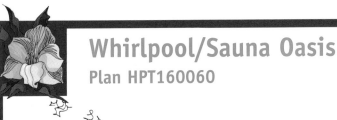

Whirlpool/Sauna Oasis
Plan HPT160060

Features At A Glance:

- *Spacious Deck Area*
- *Dry-Heat Sauna*
- *Revitalizing Whirlpool Spa*

See page 124 to order complete construction drawings for this plan.

A relaxing addition to a backyard, this sauna and whirlpool spa combination promises respite from the hectic world. Joined to the house by wood decking and a sun-filtering trellis, the dry-heat sauna has planked seating as well as a sink and shower and a bench seat in the dressing area. A small attached storage room neatly accommodates supplies and equipment.

Just outside, raised planters flank the revitalizing whirlpool spa on two sides. The third side has a long bench seat. Additional bench seating borders the wood deck on two sides. Simple lines and an open design allow this plan to blend perfectly with any style or type of house.

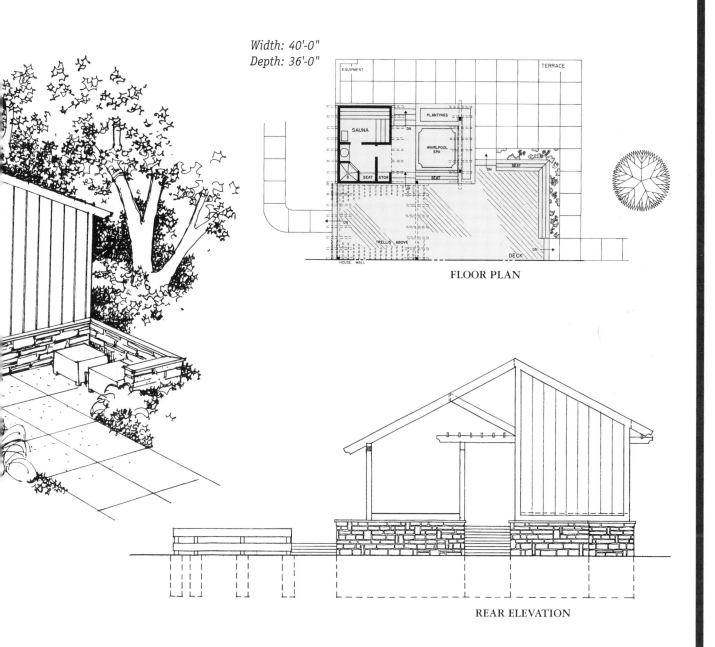

Width: 40'-0"
Depth: 36'-0"

EQUIPMENT

TERRACE

SAUNA

PLANTINGS

WHIRLPOOL
SPA

SEAT

SEAT

S

SEAT

STOR

SEAT

TRELLIS ABOVE

DECK

HOUSE WALL

FLOOR PLAN

REAR ELEVATION

Simple lines and an open design allow this plan to
blend perfectly with any style or type of house.

Covered Outdoor Kitchen
Plan HPT160061

Features At A Glance:

- *Complete Mini-Kitchen*
- *Large Brick Barbecue Grill*
- *Optional Screen Room*

See page 124 to order complete construction drawings for this plan.

In the days before modern fire protection, kitchens were established as separate buildings away from the main house for safety reasons. No longer a necessity, a separate summer kitchen is a charming option for cooking outdoors.

In this design, a spacious deck connects the barbecue area, with its generous counter space and storage, with the covered cooking area complete with sink, stove and refrigerator. Translucent panels in the roof provide lots of natural light. There is ample room under the roof for a table and chairs and you can enclose this area with screen panels to keep out flying insects. Built-in benches adjacent to the barbecue provide additional seating or serving space.

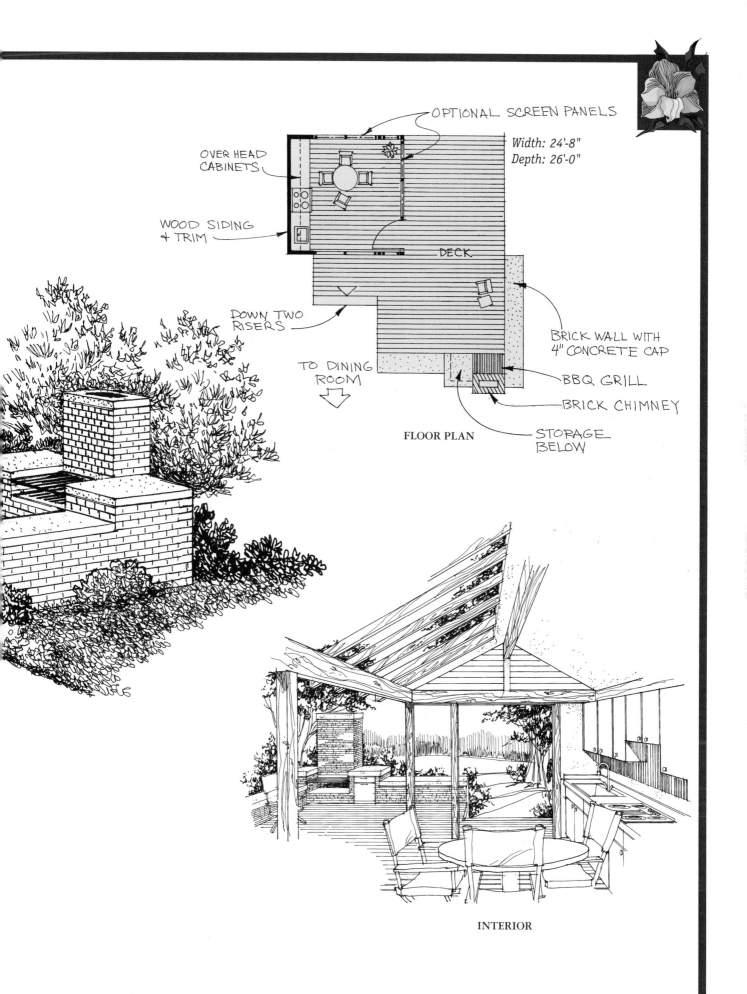

OPTIONAL SCREEN PANELS

OVER HEAD CABINETS

Width: 24'-8"
Depth: 26'-0"

WOOD SIDING + TRIM

DECK

DOWN TWO RISERS

TO DINING ROOM

BRICK WALL WITH 4" CONCRETE CAP

BBQ GRILL

BRICK CHIMNEY

STORAGE BELOW

FLOOR PLAN

INTERIOR

Enchanting Vines
Plan HPT160062

Width: 4'-3"
Depth: 6'-0"

FLOOR PLAN

Train your green vines
to grow up the sides of
these two enchanting
lattice screens.

Features At A Glance:

- *Decorates Garden*
- *A Graceful Arch*
- *Beautiful Lattice Screens*

This plan is only available on the website. Please see www.selectaplan.com for more information.

Garden-side elegance is enhanced and decorated with this gracefully made trellis. Train your green vines to grow up the sides of these two enchanting lattice screens. The wood material blends with any countryside or private garden environment—complementing farmhouse or cottage-style homes most elegantly. A beautiful curved arch binds the two screens together and tops this trellis with a definite grace. Blooming vines can continue growing over the top—creating a shaded and colorful haven for any passersby.

Garden Elegance
Plan HPT160063

Width: 7'-0"
Depth: 7'-0"

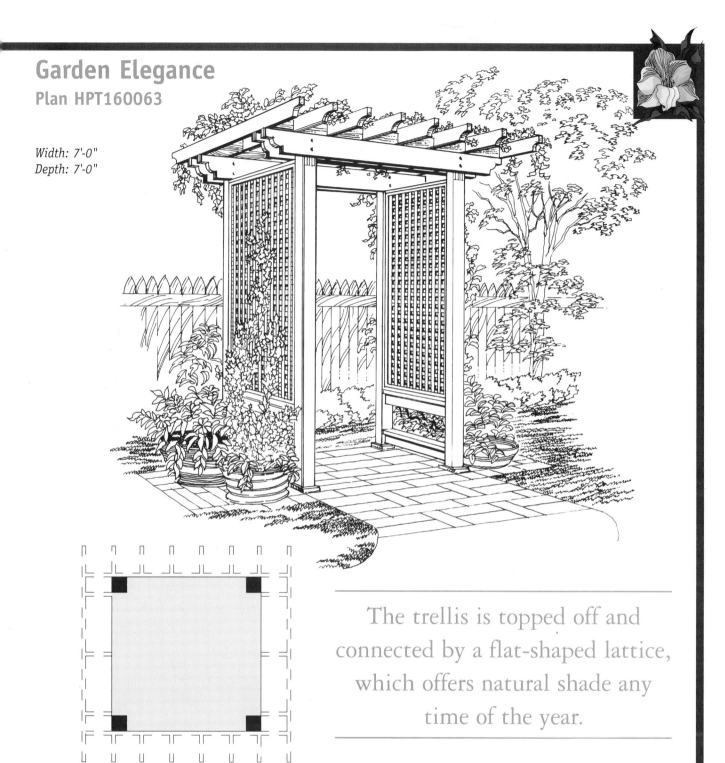

The trellis is topped off and connected by a flat-shaped lattice, which offers natural shade any time of the year.

FLOOR PLAN

Features At A Glance:

- *Enhances Any Passageway*
- *Interwoven Lattices*
- *Victorian Accents*

This plan is only available on the website. Please see www.selectaplan.com for more information.

Acting as an elegant garden portal, this stylish trellis is a beautiful addition to any private yard display. Placed at the beginning (or end) of a brick or cobblestone pathway, this structure gracefully enhances any passageway.

Green, flowering garden vines may be trained to sprawl up, down or across the interwoven side lattices. If you build with natural materials, the wooden elements will accent any rustic-made environment. Or, if you'd like, finish and paint your trellis, and bring a Victorian flavor to your garden. The trellis is topped off and connected by a flat-shaped lattice, which offers natural shade any time of the year.

Trellis Bench
Plan HPT160064

Features At A Glance:

- *Unique Design*
- *Movable Bench*
- *Easy to Build*

See page 124 to order complete construction drawings for this plan.

Build this impressive arbor to cover a garden path or walkway. Add the matching bench inside the arbor as a plant shelf or to provide shaded seating. Use the bench outside as an accent to both the arbor and the surrounding landscape. The 7'-11" patterned back and 5'-11" x 8'-10½" trellis roof are ideal for climbing vines or roses, giving this beautiful arbor even more of a garden effect.

The 8'-11" bench is wide enough to seat four or five adults comfortably. The latticework design is repeated on the back and sides of the bench. The arbor is designed to sit on a slab or you can sink the support columns right into the ground using pressure-treated materials.

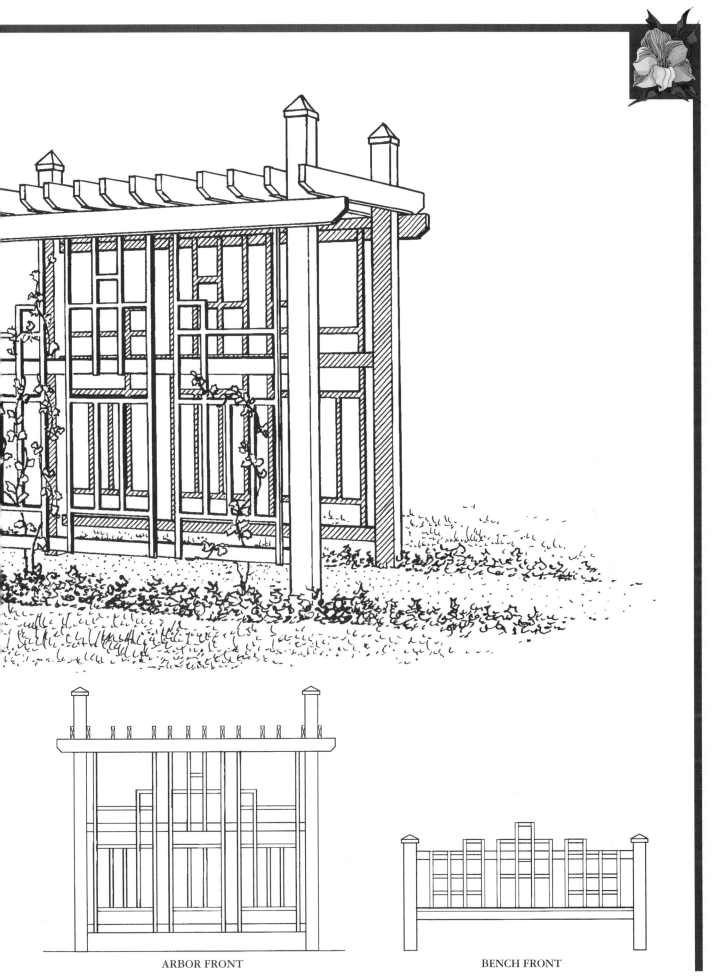

ARBOR FRONT

BENCH FRONT

Romantic Evenings
Plan HPT160065

Width: 12'-0"
Depth: 12'-9"

BENCH   BENCH

FLOOR PLAN

<hr />

Timeless elegance is the
theme to this garden beauty.

<hr />

Features At A Glance:

- *Timeless Elegance*
- *Enclosing Trellis*
- *Private Bench*

See page 124 to order complete construction drawings for this plan.

Timeless elegance is the theme to this garden beauty. One romantic evening or a comfortable leisure afternoon spent underneath this trellis will entice anyone to relax and enjoy more fresh-air outings into your own backyard.

Constructed with wood-screened lattices on every side, this enclosed, shaded haven provides a peaceful escape into the outdoors. Flowering vines can be trained to grow along the sides or above to offer extra shade, a touch of perfume and an enchanting atmosphere.

Peaceful Seclusion
Plan HPT160066

Width: 8'-8"
Depth: 2'-8"

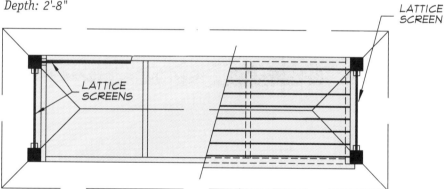

FLOOR PLAN

LATTICE
SCREENS

LATTICE
SCREEN

Features At A Glance:

- *Enclosing Lattice Screens*
- *Shading Roof*
- *Edged-Board Bench*

This plan is only available on the website. Please see www.selectaplan.com for more information.

Enjoy the outdoors in your own backyard with this stylish trellis/bench—perfect for any yard or garden setting. This wooden design features a small touch of Victorian styling, an edged-board bench, lattice screens to train flowering vines, and a hipped, overhanging roof for shade. Spend a relaxing afternoon reading or talking with a friend in the peaceful seclusion of your own garden.

Beauty and the Bridge
Plan HPT160074

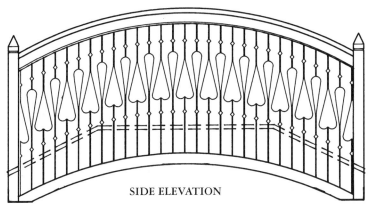

SIDE ELEVATION

Features At A Glance:

- *Funtional*
- *Decorative*
- *Three Span Lengths*

See page 124 to order complete construction drawings for this plan.

Combine form, function and beauty in this appealing bridge to enhance your landscape and provide easy passage over wet or rocky terrain. Entrance and exit ramps at either end of the bridge replicate the gentle arch of the handrail. The plans for this functional addition show how to build six-, eight- or ten-foot spans to meet your needs. The decorative railing pattern will add a touch of elegance and charm to any site.

A Bridge to the Past
Plan HPT160075

END ELEVATION

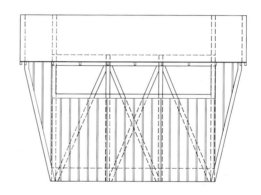

SIDE ELEVATION

Features At A Glance:

- *Historic Design*
- *Expandable Dimensions*
- *Decorative and Functional*

See page 124 to order complete construction drawings for this plan.

Nostalgia unlimited—this romantic covered bridge will re-create a unique link to history on your site. It is patterned after functional bridges built in the 1700s and 1800s, which were intended to provide a dry resting place for weary travelers. This current-day design offers expandable dimensions for a twelve-, fourteen- or sixteen-foot span. To cross a wider area, the span can be increased by multiples of those dimensions, using larger floor joists. Check with your local supplier for the span capability of the joists you employ in your project. The sides of this "glimpse into the past" have open window areas to allow air to flow freely. The generous 5'-3½" width allows for safe passage of any standard garden tractor or mower.

Yard & Garden Structures Blueprint Package

The blueprint package for these inspiring Yard and Garden Structures contains everything you need to plan and build the outdoor amenity of your choice. Some of the more complicated gazebos and lawn-shed packages will have several sheets to thoroughly explain how the structure will go together. The simpler structures such as bridges and arbors have fewer sheets. To help you further understand the process of constructing an outdoor structure, we also offer a separate package—Gazebo Construction Details—which outlines general information for construction of gazebos and similar outdoor amenities. Included are numerous illustrations, an explanation of building terms, and general tips and hints to make your building project progress smoothly.

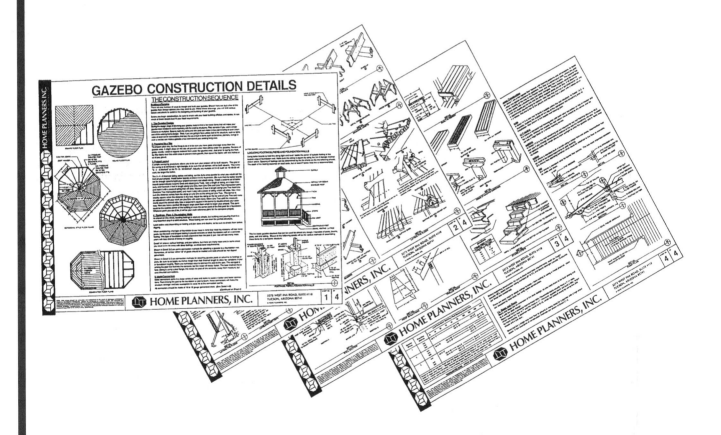

Gazebo Construction Details

This set of 24"x18" sheets contains a wealth of valuable information for gazebos and other outdoor building projects. Included are the steps of the building process; an explanation of terms; details for locating footings, piers, and foundations; information about attaching posts to piers or footings and creating free-standing benches; and much, much more. These sheets will facilitate many different outdoor construction projects for the do-it-yourselfer and will make working with contractors and subcontractors more comfortable.

Only $14.95

Or buy the Complete Construction Set which includes plans for the Yard or Garden Structure of your choice plus the Gazebo Construction Details—see page 126 for price information.

Yard & Garden Structure Plans

The plans for our Yard and Garden Structures have been custom-created by a professional designer. Among the helpful sheets for building your structure may be such information as:

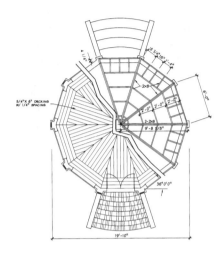

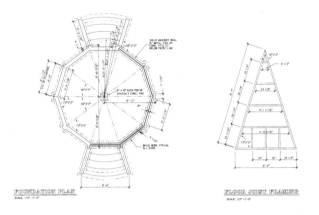

Floor Plan

Done in ½" = 1' scale, this sheet shows the exact floor plan of the structure with dimensions, flooring patterns and window and door call-outs. Details found on other sheets may also be referenced on this sheet.

Foundation and Joist Details/Materials List

This schematic of the foundation and floor and rafter joists, done in ¼" = 1' or ½" = 1' scale, gives dimensions and shows how to pour or construct the foundation and flooring components. The materials list is invaluable for estimating and planning work and acts as an accurate "shopping list" for the do-it-yourselfer.

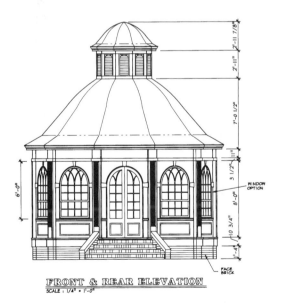

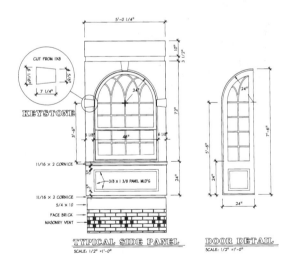

Elevations and Framing Plans/Wall Sections

Shown in ¼" = 1' or ½" = 1' scale, these helpful drawings show various views of the structure plus a complete framing plan for the flooring. Wall sections provide stud sizes, connector types, and rafter and roofing materials. They may also show moldings or other trim pieces.

Details

Cut-out details, shown in ¼" = 1' or 1" = 1' scale, are given for items such as pilaster framing, doors, side panels and rafter profiles. These details provide additional information and enhance your understanding of other aspects of the plans.

TO ORDER, CALL TOLL FREE 1-800-521-6797

Yard & Garden Structures Price Index

BLUEPRINT PRICE SCHEDULE
Prices guaranteed through December 31, 2001

TIERS	1-SET STUDY PACKAGE	4-SET BUILDING PACKAGE	8-SET BUILDING PACKAGE	1-SET REPRODUCIBLE
P1	$20	$50	$90	$140
P2	$40	$70	$110	$160
P3	$60	$90	$130	$180
P4	$80	$110	$150	$200
P5	$100	$130	$170	$230
P6	$120	$150	$190	$250
A1	$420	$460	$520	$625

Please see www.selectaplan.com for ordering

OPTIONS FOR PLANS IN TIERS P1–P6

Additional Identical Blueprints in same order for "P1–P6" price plans ....$10 per set

Reverse Blueprints (mirror image) for "P1–P6" price plans ....$10 per set

1 Set of Deck Construction Details ....$14.95 each

Deck Construction Package ....add $10 to Building Package price
  (includes 1 set of "P1–P6" price plans, plus
  1 set Standard Deck Construction Details)

1 Set of Gazebo Construction Details ....$14.95 each

Gazebo Construction Package ....add $10 to Building Package price
  (includes 1 set of "P1–P6" price plans, plus
  1 set Standard Gazebo Construction Details)

OPTIONS FOR PLANS IN TIER A1

Additional Identical Blueprints in same order for "A1" price plans ....$50 per set

Reverse Blueprints (mirror image) with 4- or 8-set order
  for "A1" price plans ....$50 fee per order

Specification Outlines ....$10 each

Materials Lists for "A1" price plans...$60 each

IMPORTANT NOTES

The 1-set study package is marked "not for construction."
Prices for 4- or 8-set Building Packages honored only at time of original order. Right-reading reverse blueprints, if available, will incur a $165 surcharge.

Yard & Garden Structures
Blueprint Order Form

TO ORDER: Find the Plan number in the Plans Index (opposite). Consult the Price Schedule (opposite) to determine the price of your plan, adding any additional or reverse sets you desire. Or specify the Complete Construction Package, which contains 1 set of Custom Plans of your choice, plus 1 set of Gazebo Construction Details. Complete the order form on this page and mail with your check or money order. Please include the correct postage and handling fees. If you prefer, you can also use a credit card and call our toll-free number, 1-800-521-6797, to place your order.

Our Service Policy
We try to process and ship every order from our office within two business days. For this reason, we won't send a formal notice acknowledging receipt of your order.

Our Exchange Policy
Since blueprints are printed in response to your order, we cannot honor requests for refunds. However, we will exchange your entire first order for an equal or greater number of blueprints within our plan collection within 90 days of the original order. The entire content of your original order must be returned to our offices before an exchange will be processed. If the returned blueprints look used, redlined or copied, we will not honor your exchange. Fees for exchanging your blueprints are as follows: 20% of the amount of the original order...*plus* the difference in cost if exchanging for a design in a higher price bracket or less the difference in cost if exchanging for a design in lower price bracket. **(Reproducible blueprints are not exchangeable.)** Please add $8.00 for postage and handling via Regular Service; $12.00 via Priority Service; $22.00 via Express Service. Shipping and handling charges are not refundable.

About Reverse Blueprints
If you want to install your structure in reverse of the plan as shown, we will include an extra set of blueprints with the images reversed for an additional fee of $10.00. Although callouts and lettering appear backward, reverses will prove useful as a visual aid if you decide to flop the plan.

How Many Blueprints Do You Need?
To study your favorite design, one set of blueprints may be sufficient. On the other hand, if you plan to use contractors or subcontractors to complete the project, you will probably need more sets. Use the checklist below to estimate the number of sets you'll need.
_____ Owner
_____ Contractor or Subcontractor
_____ Building Materials Supplier
_____ Lender or Mortgage Source, if applicable
_____ Community Building Department for Permits
            (sometimes requires 2 sets)
_____ Subdivision Committee, if any
_____ Total Number of Sets

Blueprint Hotline
Call Toll Free 1-800-521-6797. We'll ship your order within two business days. When you order by phone, please be prepared to give us the Order Form Key Number shown in the box at the bottom of the Order Form.

By FAX: Copy the order form at right and send on our FAX line: 1-800-224-6699 or 1-520-544-3086.

Canadian Customers
Order Toll Free 1-877-223-6389
For faster service and plans that are modified for building in Canada, customers may now call in orders directly to our Canadian supplier of plans and charge the purchase to a credit card. Or, you may complete the order form at right, adding the current exchange rate to all prices and mail in Canadian funds to:
Home Planners Canada

c/o Select Home Designs
301-611 Alexander Street
Vancouver, B.C., Canada V6A 1E1

By Fax: Copy the Order Form at right and send it via our Canadian FAX line: 1-800-224-6699.

BLUEPRINTS ARE NOT RETURNABLE

HOME PLANNERS, LLC
WHOLLY OWNED BY HANLEY-WOOD, LLC
3275 WEST INA ROAD, SUITE 110
TUCSON, ARIZONA 85741

Please rush me the following:
_____ Set(s) of Custom Plan _____
        (See index and Price Schedule) $ _____
_____ Additional identical blueprints in
        same order $10 per set. $ _____

_____ Reverse blueprints at $10 per set. $ _____
_____ Sets of Gazebo Construction Details
        at $14.95 per set. $ _____
_____ Sets of Complete Construction Package (Best Buy!)
        Includes Custom Plan _____
        Plus Gazebo Construction Details $ _____

POSTAGE AND HANDLING

Carrier Delivery (Requires street address—No P.O. Boxes)		
• Regular Service (Allow 7–10 business days delivery)	$8.00	$ _____
• Priority (Allow 4–5 business days delivery)	$12.00	$ _____
• Express (Allow 3 business days delivery)	$22.00	$ _____
Canada and Overseas Delivery	Phone, FAX or Mail for Quote	

NOTE: All delivery times are from date blueprint package is shipped.

POSTAGE (from box above) $ _____
SUBTOTAL $ _____
SALES TAX (AZ & MI residents, please add
appropriate state and local sales tax.) $ _____
TOTAL (Subtotal and Tax) $ _____

YOUR ADDRESS (please print)
Name _____
Street_____
City _____ State _____ ZIP _____
Daytime telephone number (_____) _____

FOR CREDIT CARD ORDERS ONLY
Please fill in the information below:

Credit card number _____

Exp. Date: Month/Year_____

Check One: ☐ Visa ☐ MasterCard ☐ Discover Card ☐ American Express

Signature _____

ORDER TOLL FREE
1-800-521-6797
OR 520-297-8200

Order Form Key
HPT16

Useful Finishing Sources

Architectural Antiques Exchange
715 N. Second St.
Philadelphia, PA 19123
(215) 922-3669
FAX (215) 922-3680
doors, entryways, fencing & gates, windows, mantels, bars, backbars, vintage plumbing

Blue Ox Millworks
Foot of X St.
Eureka, CA 95501-0847
(800) 248-4259 (707) 444-3437
FAX (707) 444-0918
balusters, baseboards, doors & windows, gutters, moldings, porches, posts, vergeboards, wainscoting

Cain Architectural Art Glass
Rt. 1 Box AAA
Bremo Bluff, VA 23022
(804) 842-3984
FAX (804) 842-1021
beveled glass, windows, custom beveling on traditional machinery

Classic Architectural Specialties
12201 Currency Circle
Forney, TX 75126
(800) 662-1221
FAX (972) 552-9054
uncommon architectural features

Creative Openings
929 N. State St.
Bellingham, WA 98225
(360) 671-6420
FAX (360) 671-0207

Cumberland Woodcraft Co.
P.O. Drawer 609
Carlisle, PA 17013
(800) 367-1884 (outside of PA)
(717) 243-0063
FAX (717) 243-6502
balusters, brackets, carvings, corbels, doors, fretwork, moldings, screened doors

Custom Ironwork, Inc.
P.O. Box 180
Union, KY 41091
(859) 384-4122
FAX (859) 384-4848
fencing & gates

Denninger Cupolas & Weathervanes
77 Whipple Rd.
Middletown, NY 10940
(845) 343-2229 (Phone and Fax)
Internet site: www.denninger.com
cupolas, weather vanes, finials, caps

Focal Point Inc.
3006 Anaconda Dr.
Tarboro, NC 27886
(800) 662-5550
FAX (800) 352-9049
arches, centerpieces, door & window casings, entryways, festoons, friezes, keystones, medallions, moldings, rosettes

Gothom, Inc.
Box 421, 110 Main St.
Erin, ONT N0B IT0 Canada
(519) 371-8345
FAX (519) 371-8268
balusters, porches, posts, screened doors, vergeboards

Mad River Woodworks Co.
Box 1067
Blue Lake, CA 95525-1067
(707) 668-5671
FAX (707) 668-5673
brackets, drops, entryways, finials, moldings, posts, spandrels, wainscoting, siding, shingles

Ornamental Mouldings Limited
P.O. Box 336
Waterloo, ONT N2J 4A4 Canada
(519) 884-4080
FAX (519) 884-9692
baseboards, door & window casings, moldings

The Renovators Supply
Renovators Old Mill
Millers Falls, MA 01349
(800) 659-2211
FAX (413) 659-9936
classic hardware, plumbing, lighting and home decorating items

San Francisco Victoriana, Inc.
2070 Newcomb Ave.
San Francisco, CA 94124
(415) 648-0313
FAX (415) 648-2812
baseboards, brackets, centerpieces, door & window casings, festoons, medallions, moldings, pilasters, posts, rosettes, wainscoting

The Millworks Inc.
P.O. Box 2987 - HPI
Durango, CO 81302
(800) 933-3930 (970) 259-5915
FAX (970) 259-5919
arches, balusters, baseboards, brackets, carvings, door and window casings, drops, keystones, moldings, pilasters, porches, posts, screened doors, vergeboards, wainscoting, windows

Tennessee Fabricating co.
2025 York Ave.
Memphis, TN 38104
(901) 725-1548
FAX (901) 725-5954
Brackets, fencing & gates, finials, porches

Vintage Wood Works
Highway 34
P.O. Box R
Quinlan, TX 75474
(903) 356-2158
FAX (903) 356-3023
arches, balusters, brackets, corbels, drops, finials, fretwork, gable decorations, porches, posts, spandrels, vergeboards